Chinese Cooking

Introduction

TECHNIQUES FOR CHINESE COOKING

Preparing tasty and attractive Chinese dishes can be a rewarding experience that is easy to accomplish. There are just a few rules to keep in mind for successfully cooking most recipes: 1) Preparation and cooking are two separate procedures. 2) All ingredients should be prepared *before* any cooking is begun. 3) Paying attention to the cooking process is crucial because many of the foods are cooked over intense heat in a matter of minutes.

The Chinese have perfected a variety of cooking techniques, including stir-frying, deep-frying, braising, steaming, roasting, barbecuing and preserving. Except for stir-frying, all of these techniques are probably familiar to you. To stir-fry correctly, an understanding of its basic principles is necessary.

Stir-frying–a rapid-cooking method invented by the Chinese in ages past–is the brisk cooking of small pieces of ingredients in hot oil over intense heat for a short time, usually just for a few minutes. During cooking, the ingredients must be kept in constant motion by stirring or tossing vigorously. Once cooking is completed, the food should be removed immediately from the heat.

When stir-frying, all of the ingredients must be well organized and prepared *before the cooking is started*. They should be measured or weighed, cleaned, chopped, sliced, combined or the like. Meat, poultry, fish and vegetables should be cut into pieces of approximately the same size for even cooking. Otherwise, one ingredient may be overcooked while others remain undercooked. The stir-frying is accomplished so quickly that there is usually not time to complete any preparation steps once cooking is begun.

The intensity of the heat used for stir-frying is important. In most cases, easily controlled high heat is needed. For this reason, a gas range with its ability for instant heat control is generally more efficient for stir-frying than is an electric range.

The kind of oil used is also crucial. A vegetable oil that can be heated to a high temperature without smoking is essential. Peanut oil, corn oil, cottonseed oil and soybean oil all work well. Other kinds of fats, such as olive oil, sesame oil, butter or lard cannot be used because they have low burning points.

Due to the variables involved in stir-frying, such as kinds of foods, type of heat and the kind of cooking equipment used, cooking times given in this book should be used as guidelines—not as absolutes. Most of the recipes, for example, were tested on a gas range. Cooking times needed when using a wok on an electric range, or when using an electric wok, may vary somewhat.

UTENSILS FOR CHINESE COOKING

A reasonably equipped kitchen usually contains more than enough utensils to adequately handle Chinese cooking. However, one item you may not have, but may wish to consider purchasing, is a wok, especially if you plan to make stir-fried dishes often. Invented centuries ago, the wok is an all-purpose cooking pan used in virtually every Chinese household for almost every kind of cooking.

Traditionally, a wok was made from thin, tempered iron, and had a rounded bottom for fast, even conduction of heat. However, modern technology has brought some changes to the wok. In addition to iron, woks are now manufactured in aluminum, stainless steel and carbon steel. Woks with flat bottoms are made for use on electric ranges and on smooth-top cooking surfaces. There are electric woks with non-stick finishes and automatic thermostatic controls. On some woks, the customary thin metal handles positioned on two sides have been replaced with a single long wooden handle. This version eliminates the necessity of keeping pot holders handy at all times to pick up or steady the wok.

Woks range in size from 12 to 24 inches in diameter. The fourteen-inch size is a good choice because it can handle most stir-frying and other cooking chores without interfering with the use of other burners on the range top.

Before a new iron or carbon steel wok is used, it should be washed and seasoned. Wash it thoroughly in hot, soapy water (the first time only) and use a scouring pad, if necessary, to remove any protective coating. Rinse the wok with water and dry it completely. Rub 1 tablespoon of vegetable oil completely over the interior of the wok. Place it over low heat until hot throughout, 3 to 5 minutes; remove wok from heat and let cool.

After each use, the wok should be soaked in hot water and cleaned with a bamboo brush or a sponge. Do not clean the wok with soap or soap-treated scouring pads. Rinse the wok with water, dry it and place over low heat until all water evaporates. Then rub 1 teaspoon of vegetable oil over the inside of the wok to prevent it from rusting.

Another very useful utensil for Chinese cooking is a cleaver. While not essential, it is handy for slicing, chopping and mincing ingredients, and is especially helpful for chopping whole chickens and ducks into Chinese-style serving pieces (see page 51).

INGREDIENTS IN CHINESE COOKING

When preparing Chinese foods, you will come across many ingredients that are familiar. You will also encounter some that may be unfamiliar such as wood ears, oyster sauce or Chinese five-spice powder. Some of the items—seasonings in particular—may be available only in Chinese food markets. Before you search for an out-of-the-way specialty store, however, check your local supermarket. Many supermarkets now stock good inventories of Chinese ingredients. In addition to canned, bottled or packaged goods, many carry fresh items such as Chinese cabbage (napa or bok choy), bean sprouts, wonton and egg-roll wrappers, bean curd and Chinese-style thin egg noodles. A check of the frozen-food cases will yield additional Chinese items.

As with any other kind of cooking, choose the freshest ingredients you can find, especially when purchasing vegetables, meat, poultry or fish. The Chinese are so conscientious about cooking with the freshest possible foods that they plan their menus around the foods they find in the market—rather than planning the marketing around the menu. The glossary that follows describes many of the Chinese foods used in the recipes in this book.

GLOSSARY OF CHINESE INGREDIENTS

Bamboo shoots: tender, ivory-colored shoots of tropical bamboo plants, used separately as a vegetable and to add crispness and a slight sweetness to dishes. They are available in cans—whole or sliced—and should be rinsed with water before using.

Bean curd (also called tofu): puréed soybeans pressed to form a white custard-like cake, used as a vegetable and as an excellent source of protein. Bean curd can be used in all kinds of recipes because it readily absorbs the flavor of other foods. Bean curd is available fresh or in cans. If fresh, it should be covered with water and stored in the refrigerator.

Bean sprouts: small white shoots of the pea-like mung bean plant, used separately as a vegetable and included in a wide variety of dishes. They are available fresh or in cans. Canned sprouts should be rinsed before use to eliminate any metallic taste. Fresh or opened, unused canned sprouts should be covered with water and stored in the refrigerator.

Bean threads (also called Chinese rice vermicelli, transparent or cellophane noodles): dry, hard, white, fine noodles made from powdered mung beans. They have little flavor of their own, but readily absorb the flavors of other foods. Bean threads can be used in numerous steamed, simmered, deep-fried or stir-fried dishes. They are available in packets or small bundles.

Black beans, fermented: strongly flavored, preserved, small black soybeans. They are quite salty and are often used as a seasoning in combination with garlic. Fermented black beans are available in cans, bottles or plastic bags; they should be rinsed or soaked in water before using.

Cabbage, Chinese: there are two types of Chinese cabbages generally available in American markets. One is bok choy, which has white stalks and green, crinkled leaves. The other is napa cabbage which has elongated tightly furled leaves with wide white ribs and soft pale green tips. Both varieties need very little cooking and are often included in soups and stir-fried dishes.

Chili sauce, Chinese: a bright red, extremely spicy sauce made from crushed fresh chili peppers and salt. It is available in cans or bottles and should be used sparingly.

Egg noodles, Chinese-style: thin pasta usually made of flour, egg, water and salt. The noodles can be purchased fresh, frozen or dehydrated. They can be boiled, braised, stir-fried or deep-fried; the time and method of cooking vary with the type of noodle. Check the package for specific instructions.

Five-spice powder, Chinese: cocoa-colored, ready-mixed blend of five ground spices, usually anise seed, fennel, clove, cinnamon and ginger or pepper. It has a slightly sweet, pungent flavor and should be used sparingly.

Ginger (also called ginger root): a knobby, gnarled root, having a brown skin and whitish or light green interior. It has a fresh, pungent flavor and is used as a basic seasoning in many Chinese recipes. Ginger is available fresh or in cans. It will keep for weeks in the refrigerator wrapped in plastic or for months if kept in salted water or dry sherry. Always remove the outer brown skin from fresh ginger before using in any recipe.

Lily buds (also called tiger-lily buds or golden needles): long, yellow strips which are the flower buds of the tiger lily. They come dried and must be soaked in warm water before using. Lily buds have a slightly musky flavor and are used in soups, stews and vegetarian dishes. They are available in cellophane packages but can be difficult to find; if you can't get them simply omit them from the recipe.

Lychee (also called lichee or litchi): a small, juicy, oval-shaped fruit with a brownish or bright red skin, white pulp and large pit. They are used in main dishes in combination with other foods or served separately as a dessert or snack. Lychees are available in cans—whole, pitted and packed in syrup.

Mushrooms, dried: dehydrated black or brown mushrooms from the Orient, having caps from 1 to 3 inches in diameter. They have a strong, distinctive flavor and are included in many different kinds of recipes. Chinese dried mushrooms must be soaked in hot water before using; they are usually thinly sliced prior to combining them with other foods. Dried mushrooms are available in cellophane packages.

Oyster sauce: a thick, brown, concentrated sauce made of ground oysters, soy sauce and brine. It imparts very little fish flavor and is used as a seasoning to intensify other flavors. Oyster sauce is included in a variety of recipes, especially in stir-fried Cantonese dishes.

Parsley, Chinese (also called cilantro or fresh coriander): a strongly flavored green herb with flat broad leaves similar in appearance to Italian or flat-leaf parsley. Commonly used fresh as a seasoning or garnish.

Peanut oil: a golden-colored oil pressed from peanuts which has a light and slightly nutty flavor. This oil has a high smoking point which makes it ideal for using in stir-fried recipes. It is available in bottles or cans.

Satay (Saté) sauce (also called Chinese barbecue sauce): a dark brown, hot, spicy sauce composed of soy sauce, ground shrimp, chili peppers, sugar, garlic, oil and spices. It is available in cans or jars.

Sesame oil: an amber-colored oil pressed from toasted sesame seeds. It has a strong, nut-like flavor and is best used sparingly. Sesame oil is generally used as a flavoring, not as a cooking oil because of its low smoking point. It is available in bottles.

Snow peas: (also called pea pods or Chinese peas): flat, green pods that are picked before the peas have matured. They add crispness, color and flavor to foods, require very little cooking and are frequently used in stir-fried dishes. Snow peas are available fresh or frozen.

Soy sauce: a pungent, brown, salty liquid made of fermented soybeans, wheat, yeast, salt and, sometimes, sugar. It is an essential ingredient in Chinese cooking. There are several types of soy sauces (light, dark, heavy), as well as Japanese-style soy sauce. The Japanese style soy sauce is somewhere between light and dark varieties. All types of soy sauce are available in bottles.

Szechuan (Sichuan) pepper: a reddish-brown pepper with a strong, pungent aroma and flavor with a time-delayed action—its potent flavor may not be noticed immediately. It should be used sparingly. It is usually sold whole or crushed in small packages.

Water chestnut: a walnut-sized bulb from an aquatic plant. The bulb has a tough, brown skin and crisp white interior. Water chestnuts are served separately as a vegetable and are used to add crisp texture and delicate sweet flavor to dishes. They are available fresh or in cans.

Wood ears (also called tree ears or cloud ears): a dried fungus that expands to five or six times its dehydrated size when soaked in warm water. They have a delicate flavor and crunchy texture and are most often used in soups. They are available in cellophane packages.

Appetizers & Soups

Pot Stickers

2 cups all-purpose flour
¾ cup plus 2 tablespoons boiling water
½ cup very finely chopped napa cabbage
8 ounces lean ground pork
2 tablespoons finely chopped water chestnuts
1 green onion, finely chopped
1½ teaspoons soy sauce

1½ teaspoons dry sherry
½ teaspoon minced fresh ginger
1½ teaspoons cornstarch
½ teaspoon sesame oil
¼ teaspoon sugar
2 tablespoons vegetable oil, divided
⅔ cup chicken broth, divided
Soy sauce, vinegar and chili oil

1. Place flour in large bowl and make a well in center. Pour in boiling water; stir with wooden spoon until dough begins to hold together. Knead dough until smooth and satiny on lightly floured surface, about 5 minutes. Cover and let rest 30 minutes.

2. For filling, squeeze cabbage to remove as much moisture as possible; place in large bowl. Add pork, water chestnuts, onion, soy sauce, sherry, ginger, cornstarch, sesame oil and sugar; mix well.

3. Divide dough into 2 equal portions; cover 1 portion with plastic wrap or a clean towel while you work with the other portion. Roll out dough to ⅛ inch thickness on lightly floured work surface. Cut out 3-inch circles with round cookie cutter or clean can. Place 1 rounded teaspoon filling in center of each dough circle.

Pot Stickers

4. To shape each pot sticker, lightly moisten edges of dough circle with water; fold in half. Starting at one end, pinch curled edges together making 4 pleats along edge. Set dumpling down firmly seam-side up. Cover finished pot stickers while you make remaining dumplings. (Cook dumplings immediately, refrigerate for up to 4 hours or freeze in resealable plastic bag.)

5. To cook pot stickers, heat 1 tablespoon of the vegetable oil in large nonstick skillet over medium heat. Set ½ of pot stickers in pan seam-side up. (If cooking frozen dumplings, do not thaw.) Cook until bottoms are golden brown, 5 to 6 minutes. Pour in ⅓ cup of the chicken broth. Cover tightly, reduce heat and cook until all liquid is absorbed, about 10 minutes (15 minutes if frozen). Repeat with remaining vegetable oil, pot stickers and chicken broth.

6. Place pot stickers browned-side up on serving platter. Serve with soy sauce, vinegar and chili oil for dipping. *Makes 32 pot stickers*

Stuffed Mushrooms

24 fresh medium mushrooms
(about 1 pound)
6 ounces boneless lean pork
¼ cup whole water chestnuts
(¼ of 8-ounce can)
3 green onions
½ small red or green bell pepper
1 small stalk celery
1 teaspoon cornstarch

1 teaspoon minced fresh ginger
2 teaspoons dry sherry
1 teaspoon soy sauce
½ teaspoon hoisin sauce
1 egg white
Vegetable oil for frying
Batter (recipe follows)
½ cup all-purpose flour

1. Clean mushrooms by wiping with a damp paper towel. Remove stems; chop stems finely and transfer to large bowl.

2. Finely chop pork, water chestnuts, onions, red pepper and celery with cleaver or food processor. Add to chopped mushroom stems. Add cornstarch, ginger, sherry, soy sauce, hoisin sauce and egg white; mix well.

3. Spoon pork mixture into mushroom caps, mounding in center. Heat oil in wok or large skillet over high heat to 375°F.

4. Prepare Batter. Dip mushrooms in flour, then in batter, coating completely. Cook 6 to 8 mushrooms at a time until golden, about 5 minutes. Drain on paper towels.   *Makes 2 dozen*

Batter

½ cup cornstarch
½ cup all-purpose flour
1½ teaspoons baking powder

¾ teaspoon salt
⅓ cup milk
⅓ cup water

Combine cornstarch, flour, baking powder and salt in medium bowl. Stir in milk and water; blend well.

Wonton Soup

½ cup finely chopped cabbage
4 ounces shelled, deveined
shrimp, finely chopped
8 ounces lean ground pork
3 green onions, finely chopped
1 egg, lightly beaten
1½ tablespoons cornstarch
2 teaspoons soy sauce
1 teaspoon oyster sauce
2 teaspoons sesame oil, divided

48 wonton wrappers
(about 1 pound)
1 egg white, lightly beaten
¾ pound bok choy or napa
cabbage
6 cups chicken broth
1 cup thinly sliced Barbecued
Pork (see page 20)
3 green onions, thinly sliced

Wonton Soup

1. For filling, squeeze cabbage to remove as much moisture as possible. Place cabbage in large bowl. Add shrimp, pork, chopped onions, whole egg, cornstarch, soy sauce, oyster sauce and 1½ teaspoons of the sesame oil; mix well.

2. For wontons, work with about 12 wrappers at a time keeping remaining wrappers covered with plastic wrap. Place 1 wonton wrapper on work surface with one point facing you. Mound 1 teaspoon filling in bottom corner. Fold bottom corner over filling.

3. Moisten side corners with egg white. Bring side corners together, overlapping slightly. Pinch together firmly to seal. Cover finished wontons with plastic wrap while you fill remaining wontons. (Cook immediately, refrigerate up to 8 hours or freeze in resealable plastic bag.)

4. Cut bok choy stems into 1-inch thick slices; cut leaves in half crosswise.

5. Cook wontons in large pot of boiling water until filling is no longer pink, about 4 minutes (6 minutes if frozen). Drain, then place in bowl of cold water to prevent wontons from sticking together.

6. Bring chicken broth to a boil in large saucepan. Add bok choy and remaining ½ teaspoon sesame oil; cook 2 minutes. Drain wontons and add to hot broth. Add slices of Barbecued Pork and sliced onions.

Makes 6 servings

Hors d'Oeuvre Rolls

Hors d'Oeuvre Rolls

½ cup Chinese-style thin egg
   noodles, broken into 1-inch
   pieces
2 tablespoons butter or
   margarine
4 ounces boneless lean pork,
   finely chopped
6 medium fresh mushrooms,
   finely chopped
6 green onions, finely chopped
8 ounces shelled, deveined
   shrimp, cooked and finely
   chopped

1 hard-cooked egg, finely
   chopped
1½ tablespoons dry sherry
½ teaspoon salt
⅛ teaspoon pepper
2 sheets commercial puff pastry
   dough or 40 wonton
   wrappers
1 egg, beaten
   Vegetable oil for frying
   Sweet and Sour Sauce (see
   page 19), optional

1. Cook noodles according to package directions until tender but still firm, 2 to 3 minutes. Drain and rinse under cold running water and drain again. Chop noodles finely.

2. Heat butter in wok or large skillet over medium-high heat. Add pork and stir-fry until browned, about 5 minutes. Add mushrooms and onions; stir-fry 2 minutes. Remove from heat and add shrimp, hard-cooked egg, cooked noodles, sherry, salt and pepper; mix well.

3. If using puff pastry, roll and trim each sheet into a 15×12-inch rectangle. Cut each rectangle into 20 (3-inch) squares.

4. Place 1 tablespoon pork mixture across center of each pastry square or wonton wrapper. Brush edges lightly with beaten egg. Roll up tightly around filling and pinch edges slightly to seal.

5. Heat oil in wok or large skillet to 375°F. Cook 6 to 8 rolls at a time until golden and crisp, 3 to 5 minutes. Drain on paper towels. Serve with Sweet and Sour Sauce, if desired. *Makes 40 rolls*

Chicken and Corn Soup

6¾ cups water, divided
  2 pounds chicken pieces
  1 medium yellow onion, thinly sliced
  1 piece fresh ginger (about 1-inch square), pared and thinly sliced
  6 whole peppercorns
1½ teaspoons salt, divided
  1 or 2 sprigs fresh parsley
  8 green onions
  1 can (16 ounces) cream-style corn

  2 teaspoons instant chicken bouillon granules
  1 teaspoon sesame oil
  ½ teaspoon minced fresh ginger
  ⅛ teaspoon ground pepper
  ¼ cup cornstarch
  2 egg whites
  2 slices cooked ham (about 1 ounce each), cut into 1½-inch strips

1. Combine 6 cups of the water, the chicken pieces, yellow onion, sliced ginger, peppercorns, 1 teaspoon of the salt and the parsley in 5-quart stockpot or Dutch oven. Bring to a boil; reduce heat to low, cover and simmer 1½ hours. Remove any scum or fat from top of stock.

2. Strain stock; return to stockpot. Cut meat from bones and shred with cleaver or knife to yield 1 cup shredded chicken.

3. Finely chop 4 of the green onions. Add chopped onions, corn, bouillon granules, sesame oil, minced ginger, pepper and remaining ½ teaspoon salt to stock. Bring to a boil.

4. Blend cornstarch with ½ cup of the remaining water in small cup. Stir into soup; cook and stir until soup thickens.

5. Beat egg whites and remaining ¼ cup water in small bowl. Stirring constantly, drizzle egg mixture slowly into soup. Stir in ham and shredded chicken.

6. Cut remaining 4 onions into thin slices. Pour soup into bowls; sprinkle with onions. *Makes 6 to 8 servings*

Chicken and Banana Squares

2 whole boneless, skinless
   chicken breasts, cooked
2 ripe medium bananas
6 slices white sandwich bread,
   trimmed and quartered
4 eggs

½ cup milk
½ cup all-purpose flour
4 cups soft bread crumbs
   (10 to 12 bread slices)
Vegetable oil for frying

1. Cut chicken breasts into 8 pieces, then cut each of those pieces into thirds, yielding 24 pieces total.

2. Cut each banana lengthwise into quarters. Cut each quarter into thirds, yielding 24 pieces total.

3. Beat eggs and milk in medium bowl until blended. Brush one side of the 24 bread pieces with egg mixture. Place 1 piece of chicken and 1 piece of banana on each egg-glazed bread piece.

4. Place flour in one bowl and soft bread crumbs in another. Coat each chicken-banana square lightly with flour, dip in egg mixture, then coat with bread crumbs. Dip in egg mixture again and coat with crumbs.

5. Heat oil in wok or large skillet over high heat to 375°F. Cook 4 to 6 squares at a time until golden, 2 to 3 minutes. Drain on paper towels.

Makes 2 dozen

Fried Wontons

1 ounce dried mushrooms
1 pound boneless lean pork
4 ounces fresh spinach
1½ tablespoons dry sherry
4 teaspoons soy sauce, divided
¼ teaspoon pepper
48 wonton wrappers
   (about 1 pound)
1 can (6 ounces) pineapple juice

½ cup distilled white vinegar
1 tablespoon catsup
½ cup sugar
1½ tablespoons cornstarch
¼ cup water
½ cup Chinese Mixed Pickled
   Vegetables (see page 80)
Vegetable oil for frying

1. Place mushrooms in bowl and cover with hot water. Let stand 30 minutes. Drain and squeeze out excess water. Cut off and discard stems.

2. Finely chop pork, spinach and mushrooms with cleaver or food processor; transfer to large bowl. Add sherry, 2 teaspoons of the soy sauce and the pepper; mix well.

Fried Wontons

3. For wontons, work with about 12 wrappers at a time keeping remaining wrappers covered with plastic wrap. Spoon 1 rounded teaspoon pork mixture onto center of each wonton wrapper. Gather edges around filling, pressing firmly at top to seal.

4. Combine pineapple juice, vinegar, catsup, sugar and remaining 2 teaspoons soy sauce in small saucepan. Bring to a boil. Blend cornstarch and water in small cup; stir into pineapple mixture. Reduce heat; cook and stir until thickened, about 3 minutes. Stir in Chinese Mixed Pickled Vegetables; keep warm.

5. Heat oil in wok or large skillet over medium-high heat to 375°F. Cook 8 to 10 wontons at a time until golden and crisp, 2 to 3 minutes. Drain on paper towels. To serve, pour pineapple mixture over wontons.　　*Makes 4 dozen*

Long Soup

1½ tablespoons vegetable oil
8 ounces boneless lean pork, cut into thin strips
4 to 6 ounces cabbage (¼ of small head), shredded
6 cups chicken broth

2 tablespoons soy sauce
½ teaspoon minced fresh ginger
4 ounces Chinese-style thin egg noodles
8 green onions, diagonally cut into ½-inch slices

1. Heat oil in wok or large skillet over medium-high heat. Add pork and cabbage; stir-fry until pork is cooked through and no longer pink, about 5 minutes.

2. Add chicken broth, soy sauce and ginger to wok. Bring to a boil; reduce heat and simmer 10 minutes.

3. Stir in noodles and onions. Cook just until noodles are tender, 1 to 4 minutes.   *Makes about 4 servings*

Long Soup

Shrimp Toast

Shrimp Toast

12 large shrimp, shelled and
    deveined, leaving tails intact
1 egg
2½ tablespoons cornstarch
¼ teaspoon salt
    Pinch pepper
3 slices white sandwich bread,
    crusts removed and
    quartered

1 hard-cooked egg yolk, cut into
    ½-inch pieces
1 slice cooked ham, cut into
    ½-inch pieces
1 green onion, finely chopped
    Vegetable oil for frying

1. Cut down back of shrimp; press gently to flatten. Beat the 1 egg,
cornstarch, salt and pepper in large bowl until blended. Add shrimp to egg
mixture; toss to coat well.

2. Place 1 shrimp cut-side down on each bread piece. Press shrimp gently into
bread. Brush or rub small amount of egg mixture over each shrimp.

3. Place 1 piece each of egg yolk and ham and a scant ¼ teaspoon onion on
top of each shrimp.

4. Heat oil in wok or large skillet over medium-high heat to 375°F. Cook 3 or
4 shrimp-bread pieces at a time until golden, 1 to 2 minutes on each side.
Drain on paper towels.   *Makes 1 dozen*

Ham and Chicken Rolls

2 whole boneless, skinless
   chicken breasts
½ teaspoon salt
¼ teaspoon pepper
¼ teaspoon Chinese five-spice
   powder
⅛ teaspoon garlic powder

4 slices cooked ham
   (about 1 ounce each)
1 egg, beaten
2 tablespoons milk
¼ cup all-purpose flour
4 spring roll or egg roll wrappers
   Vegetable oil for frying

1. Cut each chicken breast in half. Using a mallet or rolling pin, pound chicken breasts until very thin.

2. Combine salt, pepper, five-spice powder and garlic powder in small bowl. Sprinkle about ¼ teaspoon spice mixture over each flattened chicken breast.

3. Tightly roll up each ham slice and place on top of chicken; roll chicken around ham, tucking in ends.

4. Combine egg and milk in shallow dish. Coat each chicken piece lightly with flour, then dip into egg-milk mixture. Place each piece diagonally onto a spring roll wrapper. Roll up securely, folding in ends. Brush end corner with egg mixture and pinch to seal.

5. Heat oil in wok or large skillet over high heat to 375°F. Cook 3 or 4 rolls at a time until golden and chicken is cooked through, about 5 minutes. Drain on paper towels. Cool slightly. Cut into 1-inch diagonal slices to serve.

Makes 4 rolls

Hot and Sour Soup

3 dried wood ears or 4 dried
   mushrooms
20 dried lily buds, optional
1 boneless, skinless chicken
   breast half
1 tablespoon dry sherry
4 cups chicken broth
½ cup sliced bamboo shoots (½
   of 8-ounce can), drained and
   cut into matchstick pieces
4 ounces bean curd, drained and
   cut into ½-inch cubes

3 tablespoons distilled white
   vinegar
1 tablespoon soy sauce
½ teaspoon ground white pepper
2 tablespoons cornstarch
3 tablespoons water
1 egg, lightly beaten
1 teaspoon sesame oil
2 green onions, cut into 1½-inch
   slivers
2 tablespoons chopped cilantro
   (Chinese parsley)

1. Place wood ears and lily buds in separate bowls; cover with hot water. Let stand 30 minutes. Drain and squeeze out excess water. Pinch out hard knobs from center of wood ears and discard. Cut wood ears into thin strips. (If using mushrooms, cut off and discard stems; cut caps into thin slices.) Cut off and discard hard tips from lily buds; tie each bud onto itself to make a knot in the middle.

2. Cut chicken crosswise into thin slices; sprinkle with sherry. Let stand 15 minutes.

3. Bring chicken broth to a boil in 3-quart saucepan. Add wood ears, lily buds, chicken and bamboo shoots. Reduce heat and simmer, uncovered, 3 minutes. Add bean curd, vinegar, soy sauce and white pepper; cook 3 minutes more.

4. Blend cornstarch and water in small cup; stir into soup. Cook, stirring, until slightly thickened. Turn off heat. Stirring constantly, slowly pour egg into soup. Stir in sesame oil and onions. Sprinkle with cilantro just before serving.

Makes 4 to 6 servings

Hot and Sour Soup

Crab Combination Soup

1 ounce dried mushrooms
3 tablespoons cornstarch
6 tablespoons water, divided
1½ tablespoons dry sherry
4 teaspoons soy sauce
1 teaspoon vegetable oil
1 egg, lightly beaten
6 cups chicken broth
6 ounces fresh or thawed frozen
  crab meat, flaked

4 ounces fresh or thawed frozen
  sea scallops, rinsed and
  thinly sliced
½ cup bamboo shoots (½ of
  8-ounce can), drained and
  cut into matchstick pieces
8 green onions, chopped
½ teaspoon minced fresh ginger
2 egg whites

1. Place mushrooms in bowl and cover with hot water. Let stand 30 minutes. Drain and squeeze out excess water. Remove and discard stems; cut caps into thin slices.

2. Combine cornstarch, 4 tablespoons of the water, the sherry and soy sauce in small bowl; mix well and set aside.

3. Heat oil in small skillet over medium-high heat. Add egg and tilt pan to cover bottom. Cook just until egg is set. Loosen edges; turn omelet and cook other side. Remove omelet from pan, roll up and cut into thin strips.

4. Pour broth into 3-quart saucepan. Bring to a boil. Stir in mushrooms, sliced egg, crab meat, scallops, bamboo shoots, onions and ginger. Bring back to a boil.

5. Stir cornstarch mixture; pour into soup. Bring back to a boil. Beat egg whites and remaining 2 tablespoons water in small bowl. Stirring constantly, drizzle egg whites slowly into soup.   *Makes 6 servings*

Gow Gees

1 ounce dried mushrooms
48 wonton wrappers
  (about 1 pound)
2 ounces shelled, deveined
  shrimp
4 ounces boneless lean pork
3 green onions

2 teaspoons soy sauce
½ teaspoon minced fresh ginger
1 clove garlic, crushed
  Vegetable oil for frying
  Sweet and Sour Sauce (recipe
  follows)

1. Place mushrooms in bowl and cover with hot water. Let stand 30 minutes; drain and squeeze out excess water. Cut off and discard stems

2. Cut wonton wrappers into circles using 3-inch cookie cutter or clean can. Cover with plastic wrap.

3. Finely chop shrimp, pork, onions and mushrooms with cleaver or food processor; transfer to large bowl. Add soy sauce, ginger and garlic; mix well.

4. Place 1 level teaspoon pork mixture in center of each wonton circle. Brush edges with water. Fold circles in half over filling, pressing edges together to seal.

5. Heat oil in wok or large skillet over high heat to 375°F. Cook 8 to 10 gow gees at a time until golden, 2 to 3 minutes. Drain on paper towels. Serve with Sweet and Sour Sauce. *Makes 4 dozen*

Sweet and Sour Sauce

1 cup water
½ cup distilled white vinegar
½ cup sugar
¼ cup tomato paste
4 teaspoons cornstarch

Combine all ingredients in small saucepan. Bring to a boil over medium heat, stirring constantly. Boil and stir 1 minute.

Gow Gees

Barbecued Pork

Barbecued Pork

¼ cup soy sauce
2 tablespoons dry red wine
1 tablespoon brown sugar
1 tablespoon honey
2 teaspoons red food coloring
  (optional)
½ teaspoon ground cinnamon

1 green onion, cut in half
1 clove garlic, crushed
2 whole pork tenderloins (about
  12 ounces each), trimmed
  Green Onion Curls (recipe
  follows), for garnish

1. Combine soy sauce, wine, sugar, honey, food coloring, cinnamon, onion and garlic in large bowl. Add pork, turning tenderloins to coat completely. Cover and refrigerate 1 hour or overnight, turning meat occasionally.

2. Drain pork, reserving marinade. Place tenderloins on wire rack over a baking pan. Bake in preheated 350°F oven, turning and basting often with reserved marinade, until cooked through, about 45 minutes.

3. Remove pork from oven; cool. Cut into diagonal slices. Garnish with Green Onion Curls.

Makes about 8 appetizer servings

Green Onion Curls

6 to 8 medium green onions   **10 to 12 ice cubes**
   Cold water

1. Trim bulbs (white part) from onions; reserve for another use. Trim remaining stems (green part) to 4-inch lengths.

2. Using sharp scissors, cut each section of green stems lengthwise into very thin strips down to beginning of stems. Cut 6 to 8 strips in each stem section.

3. Fill large bowl about half full with cold water. Add green onions and ice cubes. Refrigerate until onions curl, about 1 hour. Drain and use for garnish.

Makes 6 to 8 curls

Meats

Mongolian Lamb

SESAME SAUCE
- 1 tablespoon sesame seeds
- ¼ cup soy sauce
- 1 tablespoon dry sherry
- 1 tablespoon red wine vinegar
- 1½ teaspoons sugar
- 1 clove garlic, minced
- 1 green onion, minced
- ½ teaspoon sesame oil

LAMB
- 1 pound boneless lean lamb (leg or shoulder)
- 2 small leeks, cut into 2-inch slivers
- 4 green onions, cut into 2-inch slivers
- 2 medium carrots, shredded
- 1 medium zucchini, shredded
- 1 red pepper, cut into matchstick pieces
- 1 green bell pepper, cut into matchstick pieces
- ½ small head napa cabbage, thinly sliced
- 1 cup bean sprouts
- 4 tablespoons vegetable oil, divided
- 4 slices pared fresh ginger, divided
- Chili oil, optional

1. For sauce, place sesame seeds in small frying pan. Shake over medium heat until seeds begin to pop and turn golden, about 2 minutes. Let cool. Crush seeds with mortar and pestle (or place on cutting board and crush with a rolling pin; scrape up sesame paste with knife) and transfer to small serving bowl. Add remaining sauce ingredients; mix well.

2. For lamb, slice meat across the grain into strips ¼ inch thick and 2 inches long.

3. Arrange meat and vegetables on large platter. Have Sesame Sauce, vegetable oil, ginger and chili oil near cooking area.

Mongolian Lamb

4. At serving time, heat electric griddle or wok to 350°F. Cook one serving at a time. For each serving, heat 1 tablespoon vegetable oil; add 1 slice ginger and cook 30 seconds; discard. Add ½ cup meat strips, stir-fry until lightly browned, about 1 minute. Add 2 cups assorted vegetables; stir-fry 1 minute. Drizzle with 2 tablespoons Sesame Sauce; stir-fry 30 seconds. Season with a few drops chili oil, if desired. Repeat for remaining servings.

Makes 4 servings

Mu Shu Pork

Mu Shu Pork

8 teaspoons soy sauce, divided
5 teaspoons dry sherry, divided
4 teaspoons cornstarch, divided
8 ounces boneless lean pork, cut into matchstick pieces
3 dried mushrooms
2 dried wood ears
7 teaspoons vegetable oil, divided
2 eggs, lightly beaten
1 tablespoon water
½ teaspoon sugar
1 teaspoon sesame oil
1 teaspoon minced fresh ginger
½ cup sliced bamboo shoots (½ of 8-ounce can), cut into matchstick pieces
1 small carrot, shredded
½ cup chicken broth
2 cups bean sprouts (about 4 ounces)
2 green onions, cut into 1½-inch slivers
½ cup hoisin sauce
16 Mandarin Pancakes (recipe follows)

1. For marinade, combine 2 teaspoons of the soy sauce, 2 teaspoons of the sherry and 1 teaspoon of the cornstarch in large bowl. Add pork and stir to coat. Let stand 30 minutes.

2. Place dried mushrooms and wood ears in small bowl and cover with hot water. Let stand 30 minutes. Drain and squeeze out excess water. Cut off and discard mushroom stems; cut caps into thin slices. Pinch out hard nobs from center of wood ears and discard; cut wood ears into thin strips.

3. Heat ½ teaspoon vegetable oil in small nonstick skillet over medium-high heat. Add ½ of eggs and tilt skillet to cover bottom. Cook just until egg is set. Loosen edges, turn omelet over and cook other side 5 seconds. Remove from skillet and repeat with another ½ teaspoon oil and remaining egg. When omelets are cool, cut in half. Stack halves and cut crosswise into ⅛-inch wide strips.

4. For sauce, combine remaining 6 teaspoons soy sauce, 3 teaspoons sherry and 3 teaspoons cornstarch in small bowl. Add the water, sugar and sesame oil; mix well.

5. Heat remaining 6 teaspoons vegetable oil in wok or large skillet over high heat. Add ginger and stir once. Add pork and stir-fry until meat is no longer pink, about 2 minutes. Add mushrooms, wood ears, bamboo shoots, carrot and chicken broth. Stir and toss 2 minutes. Add bean sprouts and onions; stir-fry 1 minute.

6. Stir cornstarch mixture; pour into wok and cook, stirring constantly, until sauce bubbles and thickens. Stir in omelet strips.

7. To serve, spread about 2 teaspoons hoisin sauce on each pancake. Spoon about 3 tablespoons pork mixture down center. Fold in bottom and roll up.

Makes 8 servings

Mandarin Pancakes

2 cups all-purpose flour	2 tablespoons sesame oil
¾ cup boiling water	

1. Place flour in bowl and make a well in center. Pour in boiling water; stir with wooden spoon until dough looks like lumpy meal. Press into a ball. Knead dough until smooth and satiny on lightly floured work surface, about 5 minutes. Cover with clean towel and let rest 30 minutes.

2. Roll dough into 10-inch long log. Cut into 10 equal pieces; keep covered.

3. Cut each piece of dough in half. Roll each half into a ball; flatten slightly. Roll each piece into a 3-inch circle on lightly floured work surface. Brush top of each with small amount of sesame oil. Stack 2 dough circles together, oil side in. Roll the pair together into a 6- to 7-inch circle. Repeat for remaining pieces of dough. (Keep uncooked pancakes covered while you roll out remaining dough.)

4. Heat nonstick skillet over medium-low heat. Cook pancakes, 1 pair at a time, turning every 30 seconds, until cakes are flecked with brown and feel dry, 2 to 3 minutes. (Be careful not to overcook; cakes become brittle.)

5. Remove from pan and separate into 2 pancakes while still hot. Stack on plate and keep covered while you cook remaining pancakes. Serve at once, refrigerate or freeze in resealable plastic bag. To reheat, wrap pancakes in clean towel (thaw completely, if using frozen). Steam over simmering water 5 minutes. Fold pancakes into quarters and arrange in serving basket.

Makes 20 pancakes

Sweet and Sour Pork

¼ cup soy sauce
1½ tablespoons dry sherry
2 teaspoons sugar
1 egg yolk
2 pounds boneless lean pork, cut into 1-inch pieces
10 tablespoons cornstarch, divided
3 cups plus 3 tablespoons vegetable oil, divided
1 can (20 ounces) pineapple chunks in syrup
¼ cup distilled white vinegar
3 tablespoons tomato sauce

1 cup water
1 large yellow onion, thinly sliced
8 green onions, diagonally cut into 1-inch pieces
1 red or green bell pepper, chopped
4 ounces fresh mushrooms, cut into quarters
2 stalks celery, diagonally cut into ½-inch slices
1 medium cucumber, seeded and cut into ¼-inch wide pieces

1. For marinade, combine soy sauce, sherry, sugar and egg yolk in large bowl. Add pork; mix to coat well. Cover and refrigerate 1 hour, stirring occasionally.

2. Drain pork, reserving marinade. Place 8 tablespoons of the cornstarch into large bowl. Add pork pieces; toss to coat well. Heat 3 cups of the oil in wok or large skillet over high heat to 375°F. Add ½ of pork pieces until brown, about 5 minutes. Drain on paper towels. Repeat with remaining pork.

3. Drain pineapple, reserving syrup. Combine the syrup, reserved soy sauce marinade, vinegar and tomato sauce in small bowl. Blend remaining 2 tablespoons cornstarch and the water in another small bowl.

4. Heat remaining 3 tablespoons oil in wok over high heat. Add all vegetables and stir-fry 3 minutes. Add pineapple syrup mixture and cornstarch mixture; cook and stir until sauce boils and thickens. Add pork and pineapple; stir-fry until heated through.

Makes 4 servings

Beef with Cashews

1 pound beef rump steak,
   trimmed
4 tablespoons vegetable oil,
   divided
½ cup water
4 teaspoons cornstarch
4 teaspoons soy sauce
1 teaspoon sesame oil
1 teaspoon oyster sauce

1 teaspoon Chinese chili sauce
8 green onions, cut into 1-inch
   pieces
2 cloves garlic, crushed
1 piece fresh ginger
   (about 1-inch square), pared
   and finely chopped
⅔ cup unsalted, roasted cashews
   (about 3 ounces)

1. Cut beef across the grain into thin slices about 2 inches long. Heat 2 tablespoons of the vegetable oil in wok or large skillet over high heat. Stir-fry ½ of beef until brown, 3 to 5 minutes. Remove and set aside. Repeat with remaining beef.

2. Combine water, cornstarch, soy sauce, sesame oil, oyster sauce and chili sauce in small bowl; mix well.

3. Heat remaining 2 tablespoons vegetable oil in wok over high heat. Add onions, garlic, ginger and cashews. Stir-fry 1 minute. Add meat and cornstarch mixture. Cook and stir until liquid boils and thickens.   *Makes 4 servings*

Beef with Cashews

Ginger Beef

2½ tablespoons distilled white
    vinegar
2 teaspoons sugar
½ teaspoon salt
4 ounces fresh ginger, pared and
    thinly sliced
1 pound beef tenderloin,
    trimmed
2 tablespoons dry sherry
2 teaspoons cornstarch

1 teaspoon soy sauce
3 tablespoons vegetable oil,
    divided
1 large green bell pepper, cut
    into 1-inch pieces
6 green onions, cut into 1-inch
    pieces
1 red chili pepper, cut into thin
    slices, for garnish

1. Combine vinegar, sugar and salt in small bowl; stir until sugar dissolves. Add ginger. Let stand 20 to 30 minutes, stirring occasionally.

2. Cut beef across the grain into thin slices about 1½-inches long. Combine sherry, cornstarch and soy sauce in medium bowl. Add beef; stir to coat well. Let stand 20 minutes, stirring occasionally. Drain beef, reserving marinade.

3. Heat 2 tablespoons of the oil in wok or large skillet over high heat. Add ⅓ of beef, spreading slices out so they do not overlap. Cook slices on each side just until light brown, 2 to 3 minutes. Remove and set aside. Repeat twice with remaining beef.

4. Heat remaining 1 tablespoon oil in wok. Add green pepper, onions, ginger mixture and reserved marinade. Stir-fry until vegetables are crisp-tender, 2 to 3 minutes. Return beef to wok. Cook and stir until heated through. Garnish with chili pepper, if desired. *Makes 4 servings*

Honey-Glazed Spareribs

1 side pork spareribs
    (about 2 pounds)
¼ cup plus 1 tablespoon soy
    sauce, divided
3 tablespoons hoisin sauce
3 tablespoons dry sherry, divided
1 tablespoon sugar
1 teaspoon minced fresh ginger

2 cloves garlic, minced
¼ teaspoon Chinese five-spice
    powder
2 tablespoons honey
1 tablespoon cider vinegar
    Green Onion Curls (page 24)
    for garnish

Honey-Glazed Spareribs

1. Have your butcher cut ribs down length of slab into 2 pieces so that each half is 2 to 3 inches wide. Cut between bones to make 6-inch pieces. Trim excess fat. Place ribs in heavy plastic bag.

2. For marinade, combine ¼ cup of the soy sauce, the hoisin sauce, 2 tablespoons of the sherry, the sugar, ginger, garlic and five-spice powder in small bowl; mix well. Pour marinade over ribs. Seal bag tightly and place in large bowl. Refrigerate 8 hours or overnight, turning bag occasionally.

3. Foil-line a large baking pan. Place rack in pan and place ribs on rack (reserve marinade). Bake in preheated 350°F oven 30 minutes. Turn ribs over, brush with marinade and bake until ribs are tender when pierced with fork, about 40 minutes more.

4. For glaze, combine honey, vinegar, remaining 1 tablespoon soy sauce and 1 tablespoon sherry in small bowl; mix well. Brush ½ of mixture over ribs; place under broiler 4 to 6 inches from heat source and broil until ribs are glazed, 2 to 3 minutes. Turn ribs over, brush with remaining honey mixture and broil until glazed. Cut into serving-size pieces. Garnish with Green Onion Curls, if desired. *Makes about 4 servings*

Spiced Pork

Spiced Pork

3 tablespoons soy sauce, divided
2 tablespoons cornstarch
2 tablespoons dry sherry
1 teaspoon minced fresh ginger
½ teaspoon Chinese five-spice powder
⅛ teaspoon pepper
2 pounds boneless lean pork, cut into large pieces

Vegetable oil for frying
¼ cup water
1 teaspoon instant chicken bouillon granules
Chinese Mixed Pickled Vegetables (see page 80), optional

1. Combine 2 tablespoons of the soy sauce, the cornstarch, the sherry, ginger, five-spice powder and pepper in large bowl. Add pork, one piece at a time, turning to coat well. Cover and refrigerate 1 hour, stirring occasionally.

2. Heat oil in wok or large skillet to 375°F. Cook ½ of pork until brown and cooked through, 3 to 5 minutes. Drain on paper towels. Repeat with remaining pork. Cut pork into ¼- to ½-inch wide slices. Transfer to serving dish; keep warm.

3. Combine water, bouillon granules and remaining 1 tablespoon soy sauce in small saucepan. Bring to a boil. Pour mixture over sliced pork. Garnish with Chinese Mixed Pickled Vegetables, if desired.   *Makes 4 servings*

Beef with Peppers

1 ounce dried mushrooms
1 pound beef tenderloin,
   trimmed
2½ tablespoons vegetable oil
1 clove garlic, crushed
¼ teaspoon Chinese five-spice
   powder
2 small yellow onions, cut into
   wedges

1 green bell pepper, thinly sliced
1 red bell pepper, thinly sliced
¼ cup water
1 tablespoon soy sauce
1 teaspoon cornstarch
1 teaspoon instant beef bouillon
   granules
1 teaspoon sesame oil

1. Place mushrooms in bowl and cover with hot water. Let stand 30 minutes. Drain and squeeze out excess water. Remove and discard stems; slice caps into thin strips.

2. Cut beef into thin slices 1 inch long.

3. Heat vegetable oil in wok or large skillet over high heat. Add garlic and five spice powder; stir-fry 15 seconds. Add beef and stir-fry until brown, about 5 minutes. Add onions; stir-fry 2 minutes. Add mushrooms and peppers; stir-fry until peppers are crisp-tender, about 2 minutes.

4. Combine remaining ingredients in small bowl. Stir into wok. Cook and stir until liquid boils and thickens.   *Makes 4 servings*

Beef with Noodles

Beef with Noodles

8 ounces Chinese-style thin egg noodles, cooked and drained
½ cup water
3 teaspoons soy sauce, divided
¼ teaspoon salt
2 teaspoons instant chicken bouillon granules
1 pound beef rump steak, trimmed

6 tablespoons vegetable oil, divided
6 green onions, diagonally sliced
1 piece fresh ginger (about 1 inch square), pared and thinly sliced
2 cloves garlic, crushed

1. Place a clean towel over wire cooling racks. Spread cooked noodles evenly over towel. Let dry about 3 hours.

2. Combine water, 2 teaspoons of the soy sauce, the salt and bouillon granules in small bowl. Cut beef across the grain into thin slices about 2-inches long.

3. Heat 4 tablespoons of the oil in wok or large skillet over high heat. Add noodles and stir-fry 3 minutes. Pour water mixture over noodles; toss until noodles are completely coated, about 2 minutes. Transfer noodles to serving plate; keep warm.

4. Heat remaining 2 tablespoons oil in wok over high heat. Add beef, onions, ginger, garlic and remaining 1 teaspoon soy sauce. Stir-fry until beef is cooked through, about 5 minutes. Spoon meat mixture over noodles.

Makes 4 servings

Satay Beef

1 pound beef tenderloin, trimmed	1 medium yellow onion, coarsely chopped
5 tablespoons water, divided	1 clove garlic, crushed
1 teaspoon cornstarch	1 tablespoon dry sherry
3½ teaspoons soy sauce, divided	1 tablespoon satay sauce
1 to 2 teaspoons sesame oil	1 teaspoon curry powder
2 tablespoons vegetable oil	½ teaspoon sugar

1. Cut beef across the grain into thin slices. Flatten each slice by pressing with fingers.

2. Combine 3 tablespoons of the water, the cornstarch, 1½ teaspoons of the soy sauce and the sesame oil in medium bowl. Add beef; mix to coat well. Let stand 20 minutes.

3. Heat vegetable oil in wok or large skillet over high heat. Add ½ of beef, spreading out slices so they do not overlap. Cook slices on each side just until light brown, 2 to 3 minutes. Remove and set aside. Repeat with remaining meat.

4. Add onion and garlic to wok; stir-fry until onion is soft, about 3 minutes.

5. Combine remaining 2 tablespoons water, 2 teaspoons soy sauce, the sherry, satay sauce, curry powder and sugar in small cup. Add to wok; cook and stir until liquid boils. Return beef to wok; cook and stir until heated through.

Makes 4 servings

Beef with Black Bean Sauce

1½ pounds beef rump steak,
 trimmed
2½ tablespoons soy sauce
1½ tablespoons dry sherry
 3 teaspoons cornstarch, divided
 1 egg white
⅔ cup water, divided
1½ tablespoons fermented, salted
 black beans

¼ teaspoon sugar
4 tablespoons vegetable oil,
 divided
4 green onions, cut into 1-inch
 pieces
1 red bell pepper, thinly sliced
½ cup sliced bamboo shoots
 (½ of 8-ounce can)
1 teaspoon curry powder

1. Cut beef across the grain into thin slices 2 inches long. Combine soy sauce, sherry, 1 teaspoon of the cornstarch and the egg white in medium bowl; beat lightly. Add beef; stir to coat well. Let stand 30 minutes, stirring occasionally.

2. Combine ⅓ cup of the water and the beans in small bowl. Let stand 15 minutes. Drain beans, reserving 1 teaspoon of the water. Combine beans, reserved water and the sugar on a small plate. Mash well with fork.

3. Heat 2 tablespoons of the oil in wok or large skillet over high heat. Add onions, red pepper, bamboo shoots and curry powder; stir-fry until vegetables are crisp-tender, 2 minutes. Remove and set aside.

4. Combine remaining ⅓ cup water and 2 teaspoons cornstarch in small cup. Heat remaining 2 tablespoons oil in wok over high heat. Add beef and marinade; stir-fry until beef is brown, about 5 minutes. Add vegetables and mashed beans; mix well. Stir in cornstarch mixture. Cook and stir until liquid boils and thickens. *Makes 4 servings*

Braised Lion's Head

MEATBALLS
 1 pound lean ground pork
 4 ounces shrimp, shelled,
  deveined and finely chopped
¼ cup sliced water chestnuts,
  finely chopped
 1 teaspoon minced fresh ginger
 1 green onion, finely chopped

1 tablespoon soy sauce
1 tablespoon dry sherry
½ teaspoon salt
½ teaspoon sugar
1 tablespoon cornstarch
1 egg, lightly beaten
2 tablespoons vegetable oil

SAUCE
1½ cups chicken broth
 2 tablespoons soy sauce
½ teaspoon sugar
 1 head napa cabbage
  (1½ to 2 pounds)

2 tablespoons cornstarch
3 tablespoons cold water
1 teaspoon sesame oil

Braised Lion's Head

1. For meatballs, combine all meatball ingredients except oil in large bowl; mix well. Divide mixture into 8 portions. Shape each portion into a ball.

2. Heat vegetable oil in wok or large nonstick skillet over medium-high heat. Brown meatballs, shaking or stirring occasionally so meatballs keep their shape, 6 to 8 minutes.

3. Transfer meatballs to 5-quart stockpot; discard drippings. Add chicken broth, soy sauce and sugar. Bring to a boil; reduce heat, cover and simmer 30 minutes.

4. While meatballs are cooking, core cabbage,; cut base of leaves into 2-inch squares. Cut leafy tops in half. Place cabbage over meatballs. Cover and simmer 10 minutes more.

5. Using slotted spoon, transfer cabbage and meatballs to serving platter. Blend cornstarch and water in small cup. Stirring constantly, slowly add cornstarch mixture to pan juices; cook until slightly thickened. Stir in sesame oil. To serve, pour sauce over meatballs and cabbage.

Makes 4 to 6 servings

Sherried Beef and Spinach

1 pound beef tenderloin,
   trimmed
3 tablespoons dry sherry
1½ tablespoons soy sauce
1 teaspoon sugar
½ teaspoon sesame oil
1 pound fresh spinach, trimmed
3 tablespoons vegetable oil,
   divided

1 piece fresh ginger
   (about 2×1-inch), pared and
   thinly sliced
2 tablespoons water
½ teaspoon cornstarch
1 teaspoon instant chicken
   bouillon granules

1. Cut beef across the grain into thin slices. Cut each slice in half. Flatten slightly by pressing with fingers.

2. Combine sherry, soy sauce, sugar and sesame oil in medium bowl. Add beef; mix to coat well. Cover and refrigerate 2 hours, stirring occasionally.

3. Cut spinach leaves into large pieces. If spinach has thick stems, cut them into ½-inch diagonal slices.

4. Heat 2 tablespoons of the vegetable oil in wok or large skillet over high heat. Add ginger and spinach stems and stir-fry 2 minutes. Remove and set aside.

5. Add remaining 1 tablespoon vegetable oil to wok. Drain meat, reserving marinade. Add ½ of beef to wok spreading out slices so they do not overlap. Cook slices on each side just until light brown, 2 to 3 minutes. Remove and set aside. Repeat with remaining beef.

6. Blend water, cornstarch and bouillon granules into reserved marinade; add to wok. Cook until liquid boils, 1 to 2 minutes. Add spinach leaves, stems and ginger. Stir-fry until spinach is wilted, about 3 minutes. Add beef; stir-fry until heated through, about 1 minute more.

Makes 4 servings

Two-Onion Pork Shreds

½ teaspoon Szechuan
   peppercorns
4 teaspoons soy sauce, divided
4 teaspoons dry sherry, divided
7½ teaspoons vegetable oil, divided
1 teaspoon cornstarch
8 ounces boneless lean pork
2 teaspoons red wine vinegar

½ teaspoon sugar
2 cloves garlic, crushed
½ small yellow onion, cut into
   ¼-inch slices
8 green onions, cut into 2-inch
   pieces
½ teaspoon sesame oil

1. For marinade, place peppercorns in small skillet. Shake over medium-low heat, shaking skillet often, until fragrant, about 2 minutes. Let cool. Crush peppercorns with mortar and pestle (or place between paper towels and crush with a hammer).* Transfer to medium bowl. Add 2 teaspoons of the soy sauce, 2 teaspoons of the sherry, 1½ teaspoons of the vegetable oil and the cornstarch; mix well.

2. Cut pork into ⅛-inch thick slices, then cut into 2×½-inch pieces. Add to marinade and stir to coat well. Let stand 30 minutes.

3. Combine remaining 2 teaspoons soy sauce, 2 teaspoons sherry, the vinegar and sugar in small bowl; mix well.

4. Heat remaining 6 teaspoons vegetable oil in wok or large skillet over high heat. Add garlic and stir once. Add pork and stir-fry until meat is no longer pink, about 2 minutes. Add yellow onion and stir-fry 1 minute; add green onion and stir-fry 30 seconds. Add soy-vinegar mixture and cook 30 seconds. Stir in sesame oil. *Makes 2 to 3 servings*

*Note: Szechuan peppercorns are deceptively potent. Wear rubber or plastic gloves when crushing them and do not touch your eyes or lips when handling.

Two-Onion Pork Shreds

Poultry

Kung Pao Chicken

5 teaspoons soy sauce, divided
5 teaspoons dry sherry, divided
3½ teaspoons cornstarch, divided
¼ teaspoon salt
3 boneless, skinless chicken breast halves, cut into bite-size pieces
1 tablespoon red wine vinegar
2 tablespoons chicken broth or water

1½ teaspoons sugar
3 tablespoons vegetable oil, divided
⅓ cup salted peanuts
6 to 8 small dried hot chili peppers
1½ teaspoons minced fresh ginger
2 green onions, cut into 1½-inch pieces

1. For marinade, combine 2 teaspoons of the soy sauce, 2 teaspoons of the sherry, 2 teaspoons of the cornstarch and the salt in large bowl; mix well. Add chicken; stir to coat well. Let stand 30 minutes.

2. Combine remaining 3 teaspoons soy sauce, 3 teaspoons sherry, the vinegar, chicken broth, sugar and remaining 1½ teaspoons cornstarch in small bowl; mix well and set aside.

3. Heat 1 tablespoon of the oil in wok or large skillet over medium heat. Add peanuts and cook until golden. Remove and set aside.

4. Heat remaining 2 tablespoons oil in wok over medium heat. Add chili peppers and stir-fry until peppers just begin to char, about 1 minute. Increase heat to high. Add chicken and stir-fry 2 minutes. Add ginger; stir-fry until chicken is cooked through, about 1 minute more. Add onions and peanuts to wok. Stir cornstarch mixture and add to wok; cook and stir until sauce boils and thickens.   *Makes 3 servings*

Kung Pao Chicken

Almond Chicken

1½ cups water
4 tablespoons dry sherry, divided
2½ tablespoons cornstarch, divided
4 teaspoons soy sauce
1 teaspoon instant chicken
  bouillon granules
1 egg white
½ teaspoon salt
4 whole boneless, skinless
  chicken breasts, cut into
  1-inch pieces
  Vegetable oil for frying

½ cup blanched whole almonds
  (about 3 ounces)
1 large carrot, diced
1 teaspoon minced fresh ginger
6 green onions, cut into 1-inch
  pieces
3 stalks celery, diagonally cut
  into ½-inch pieces
8 fresh mushrooms, sliced
½ cup sliced bamboo shoots
  (½ of 8-ounce can), drained

Almond Chicken

1. Combine water, 2 tablespoons of the sherry, 1½ tablespoons of the cornstarch, the soy sauce and bouillon granules in small saucepan. Cook and stir over medium heat until mixture boils and thickens, about 5 minutes. Keep warm.

2. Combine remaining 2 tablespoons sherry, 1 tablespoon cornstarch, egg white and salt in medium bowl. Add chicken pieces; stir to coat well.

3. Heat oil in wok or large skillet over high heat to 375°F. Add chicken pieces, one at a time (cook only ⅓ of the pieces at a time), and cook until light brown, 3 to 5 minutes. Drain on paper towels. Repeat with remaining chicken.

4. Remove all but 2 tablespoons oil from wok. Add almonds and stir-fry until golden, about 2 minutes; drain.

5. Add carrot and ginger; stir-fry 1 minute. Add all remaining vegetables; stir-fry until crisp-tender, about 3 minutes. Stir in chicken, almonds and sauce; cook and stir until heated through.   *Makes 4 to 6 servings*

Sesame Chicken Salad

1 tablespoon sesame seeds	3 stalks celery
3 whole chicken breasts	1 tablespoon sesame oil
6 cups water	1 tablespoon vegetable oil
2 tablespoons soy sauce, divided	¼ teaspoon ground ginger
½ teaspoon salt	⅛ teaspoon pepper
½ teaspoon Chinese five-spice powder	

1. Sprinkle sesame seeds into small shallow baking pan. Bake in preheated 350°F oven until golden, 5 to 8 minutes.

2. Combine chicken, water, 1 tablespoon of the soy sauce, the salt and five-spice powder in 3- or 4-quart saucepan. Cover and bring to a boil. Reduce heat and simmer 15 to 20 minutes. Remove from heat. Let stand until chicken is cool enough to handle, about 1 hour.

3. Using slotted spoon, remove chicken and drain (reserve broth). Remove and discard bones. Cut meat into ½-inch wide slices.

4. Cut celery into diagonal slices. Bring reserved cooking broth back to boil. Add celery and cook until crisp-tender, 1 to 2 minutes. Using slotted spoon, remove celery and drain.

5. Combine remaining 1 tablespoon soy sauce, sesame and vegetable oils, ginger and pepper in large bowl. Add chicken and celery; toss to coat well. Transfer to serving bowl. Sprinkle with toasted sesame seeds.

Makes 4 servings

Marinated Chicken Wings

3 tablespoons soy sauce
3 tablespoons dry sherry
2 tablespoons brown sugar
1 teaspoon grated fresh ginger
2 cloves garlic, crushed
6 green onions, diagonally cut
   into thin slices
1½ pounds chicken wings, tips cut
   off

2 tablespoons vegetable oil
1 can (8 ounces) sliced bamboo
   shoots, drained
4 teaspoons cornstarch
¾ cup water
1 teaspoon instant chicken
   bouillon granules

1. For marinade, combine soy sauce, sherry, sugar, ginger and garlic in large bowl. Add onions and chicken; toss to coat well. Cover and refrigerate 1 hour, stirring occasionally.

2. Heat oil in wok or large skillet over high heat. Add bamboo shoots and stir-fry 2 minutes. Remove and set aside.

3. Drain chicken and onions, reserving marinade. Add chicken and onions to wok; stir-fry over medium-high heat until chicken is brown, about 5 minutes. Reduce heat to low. Cook until chicken is tender, 15 to 20 minutes.

4. Blend cornstarch and water in small bowl. Stir in bouillon granules and reserved marinade. Add cornstarch mixture to wok. Cook over high heat until liquid boils and thickens. Stir in bamboo shoots. Cook and stir 2 minutes.

Makes 4 servings

Chinese Chicken Salad

2 whole chicken breasts
4 cups water
1 tablespoon dry sherry
2 slices pared fresh ginger
2 whole green onions
¼ cup prepared Chinese plum
   sauce
2 tablespoons distilled white
   vinegar
1 tablespoon vegetable oil
1 tablespoon sesame oil
1½ teaspoons soy sauce
1½ tablespoons sugar
1 teaspoon dry mustard

3 tablespoons slivered almonds
2 tablespoons sesame seeds
4 cups shredded iceberg lettuce
1 small carrot, shredded
1½ cups bean sprouts
   (about 3 ounces)
3 green onions, cut into 1½-inch
   slivers
¼ cup cilantro leaves (Chinese
   parsley)
   Bean threads or Vermicelli
   (page 92), cooked and
   drained

Chinese Chicken Salad

1. Combine chicken, water, sherry, ginger and whole green onions in 3-quart saucepan. Bring to a boil; reduce heat, cover and simmer 20 minutes. Remove from heat. Let stand until chicken is cool.

2. Strain stock and refrigerate or freeze for another use. Remove and discard skin and bones from chicken. Pull meat into long shreds.

3. For dressing, combine plum sauce, vinegar, vegetable and sesame oils, soy sauce, sugar and mustard in small bowl; mix well.

4. Place almonds in small dry skillet. Shake over medium heat until golden and fragrant, about 3 minutes. Transfer to large salad bowl. Toast sesame seeds in same skillet until seeds are golden and begin to pop, about 2 minutes. Add sesame seeds to almonds.

5. Add lettuce, carrot, bean sprouts, green onion slivers, cilantro and cooked chicken. Toss to coat evenly. Add bean threads and toss to mix well.

Makes 6 to 8 servings

Duck with Pineapple

Duck with Pineapple

1 ready-to-cook duck
   (4 to 5 pounds)
1¼ cups water, divided
6 tablespoons dry sherry, divided
4½ tablespoons distilled white
   vinegar, divided
4½ tablespoons soy sauce, divided
4 tablespoons American-style
   barbecue sauce, divided
¼ teaspoon Chinese five-spice
   powder

1 small ripe pineapple
1 tablespoon cornstarch
2 tablespoons vegetable oil
2 teaspoons minced fresh ginger
1 clove garlic, crushed
4 green onions, diagonally cut
   into thin slices
   Green Onion Curls (page 21),
   for garnish

1. Rinse duck and place on wire rack in large baking pan. Combine ½ cup of the water, 3 tablespoons *each* of the sherry, vinegar, soy sauce and barbecue sauce, and the ¼ teaspoon five-spice powder in medium bowl; mix well. Pour mixture over duck. Roast duck, uncovered, in preheated 425°F oven, basting and turning often, until light brown, about 20 minutes. Reduce oven temperature to 350°F and roast duck, basting and turning often, 1 hour more. Remove duck from oven; cool completely.

2. Cut duck in half. Remove and discard backbone. Cut duck into small serving-size pieces (see page 51).

3. Twist crown from pineapple. Cut pineapple lengthwise into quarters. Using curved knife, remove fruit from shells. Trim off core and cut fruit into ¼-inch slices.

4. Combine remaining ¾ cup water, 3 tablespoons sherry, 1½ tablespoons *each* vinegar and soy sauce, 1 tablespoon barbecue sauce and the cornstarch in small bowl. Heat oil in wok or large skillet over high heat. Add ginger and garlic and stir-fry 1 minute. Add duck pieces; stir-fry until duck is hot, 3 to 4 minutes. Stir water mixture and pour over duck; cook and stir until sauce boils. Add pineapple slices and onions. Cook and stir until pineapple is hot, about 2 minutes more. Garnish with Green Onion Curls, if desired.

Makes 6 servings

Honey Chili Chicken

1 broiler/fryer chicken (3 to 4 pounds)	2 teaspoons cornstarch
½ cup all-purpose flour	4 teaspoons Chinese chili sauce
½ teaspoon salt	2 teaspoons soy sauce
Vegetable oil for frying	1½ teaspoons minced fresh ginger
⅓ cup water	3 tablespoons honey
⅓ cup lemon juice	6 green onions, cut lengthwise into thin slices

1. Rinse chicken and cut into small serving-size pieces (see page 51). Combine flour and salt in large bowl. Add chicken pieces and toss to coat well.

2. Heat oil in wok or large skillet over high heat to 375°F. Add chicken, one piece at a time (cook only ⅓ of the pieces at a time), and cook until golden, about 5 minutes. Drain on paper towels. Repeat with remaining chicken.

3. Remove all but 1 tablespoon oil from wok. Combine water, lemon juice, cornstarch, chili sauce and soy sauce in small bowl; mix well.

4. Add ginger to wok; stir-fry 1 minute. Add honey; cook and stir 1 minute. Stir in cornstarch-chili mixture; cook and stir until sauce boils, about 1 minute. Stir in chicken pieces; cook and stir until heated through, about 3 minutes. Stir in onions; cook and stir 1 minute more.

Makes 4 to 6 servings

Lemon Chicken

CHICKEN
- 4 whole boneless, skinless chicken breasts
- ½ cup cornstarch
- ½ teaspoon salt
- ⅛ teaspoon pepper
- ¼ cup water
- 4 egg yolks, lightly beaten
- Vegetable oil for frying
- 4 green onions, sliced

LEMON SAUCE
- 1½ cups water
- ½ cup lemon juice
- 3½ tablespoons brown sugar
- 3 tablespoons cornstarch
- 3 tablespoons honey
- 2 teaspoons instant chicken bouillon granules
- 1 teaspoon minced fresh ginger

1. Cut chicken breasts in half. Pound with mallet or rolling pin to flatten slightly.

2. Combine cornstarch, salt and pepper in small bowl. Gradually blend in water and egg yolks.

3. Heat oil in wok or large skillet over high heat to 375°F. Dip chicken breasts, one at a time, into cornstarch-egg yolk mixture. Cook chicken breasts, two at a time, until golden, about 5 minutes. Drain on paper towels. Keep warm while cooking remaining chicken.

4. Cut each breast into three or four pieces and arrange on serving plate. Sprinkle with onions.

5. For sauce, combine all sauce ingredients in medium saucepan; mix well. Cook over medium heat, stirring constantly, until sauce boils and thickens, about 5 minutes. Pour over chicken. *Makes 4 to 6 servings*

Lemon Chicken

Tea Smoked Chicken

1 teaspoon Szechuan
   peppercorns
2 tablespoons dry sherry
2 tablespoons soy sauce
½ teaspoon granulated sugar
6 thin slices pared fresh ginger
2 green onions, cut into 2-inch
   pieces
1 teaspoon salt
1 broiler/fryer chicken
   (3 to 4 pounds)
⅓ cup black tea leaves

3 tablespoons brown sugar
⅓ cup long-grain rice
1 strip dried tangerine peel
   (about 2 inches long) or
   1 teaspoon grated orange
   peel
Mandarin Pancakes (page 25)
Prepared plum sauce or hoisin
   sauce
4 green onions, cut into 2-inch
   slivers

1. For marinade, crush peppercorns with mortar and pestle (or place between paper towels and crush with a hammer). Combine crushed peppercorns, sherry, soy sauce, granulated sugar, ginger, onion pieces and salt. Rub chicken inside and out with marinade.* Cover and refrigerate 8 hours or overnight.

2. Place chicken breast-side up on rack in large stockpot. Pour in 1½-inches water. Cover, bring to a boil, and steam until meat near thigh bone is no longer pink, about 45 to 50 minutes. Let stand until cool enough to handle. Lift chicken from rack and drain juices from cavity.

3. Line a large wok and its lid with foil. (Do not use an electric wok with nonstick finish.) For smoking, place tea leaves, brown sugar, rice and tangerine peel in bottom of foil-lined wok; mix well. Set rack on top of mixture in wok. Place chicken breast-side up on rack. Cover with foil-lined lid.

4. Cook over high heat 2 minutes. Turn off heat and leave covered 5 minutes. Repeat 2 more times. After final smoking, let stand, covered, to allow smoke to subside, about 30 minutes. Discard smoking mixture.

5. Slice chicken from bones and arrange on serving platter. Serve 1 or 2 chicken slices in Mandarin Pancake; top with plum sauce and slivered onions.

Makes 6 to 8 servings

*Note: Szechuan peppercorns are deceptively potent. Wear rubber or plastic gloves when rubbing chicken with marinade and do not touch your eyes or lips when handling peppercorns or marinade.

Tea Smoked Chicken

Hoisin Chicken

1 broiler/fryer chicken
  (3 to 4 pounds)
½ cup plus 1 tablespoon
  cornstarch, divided
  Vegetable oil for frying
2 teaspoons grated fresh ginger
2 medium yellow onions,
  chopped
8 ounces fresh broccoli, cut into
  1-inch pieces
1 red or green bell pepper,
  chopped

2 cans (4 ounces each) whole
  button mushrooms, drained
1 cup water
3 tablespoons dry sherry
3 tablespoons cider vinegar
3 tablespoons hoisin sauce
4 teaspoons soy sauce
2 teaspoons instant chicken
  bouillon granules

1. Rinse chicken and cut into small serving-size pieces (see next page). Place ½ cup of the cornstarch in large bowl. Add chicken pieces and toss to coat well.

2. Heat oil in wok or large skillet over high heat to 375°F. Add chicken pieces, one at a time (cook only about ⅓ of the chicken pieces at a time), and cook until golden and cooked through, about 5 minutes. Drain on paper towels. Repeat with remaining chicken.

3. Remove all but 2 tablespoons oil from wok. Add ginger and stir-fry 1 minute. Add onions; stir-fry 1 minute. Add broccoli, red pepper and mushrooms; stir-fry 2 minutes.

4. Combine remaining ingredients and remaining 1 tablespoon cornstarch in small bowl. Add to wok. Cook and stir until sauce boils and turns translucent. Return chicken to wok. Cook and stir until chicken is heated through, about 2 minutes.

Makes 6 servings

How to Cut Chicken Chinese-Style

Recipes for Chinese chicken dishes often instruct that chicken be cut into serving-size pieces. These pieces should be smaller than chicken pieces generally are cut. Here are the directions for cutting a whole chicken Chinese-style. A cleaver is the best utensil for chopping a chicken, although a sharp knife or poultry shears may be used.

1. Place chicken breast-side up on a heavy cutting board. Cut in half lengthwise, cutting slightly to one side of the breast bone and the backbone. Cut completely through the chicken to make two pieces. Remove and discard backbone, if desired.

2. Pull each leg up slightly from the breast section. Cut through the ball and socket joint to remove each leg.

3. Cut through the knee joint of each leg to separate into a drumstick and thigh. Pull each wing away from breast and cut through the joint next to the breast.

4. Cut each drumstick, thigh and breast piece crosswise into three pieces, cutting completely through bones. Cut each wing into two pieces.

Makes 22 small serving-size pieces

Step 1

Step 2

Step 3

Step 4

Chicken and Chinese Sausages in Clay Pot

6 dried mushrooms
2 tablespoons soy sauce
2 tablespoons dry sherry
1 teaspoon cornstarch
½ teaspoon sugar
¼ teaspoon ground white pepper
2 teaspoons minced fresh ginger, divided
6 boneless, skinless chicken thighs, cut into 1½-inch pieces

1 tablespoon vegetable oil
1 clove garlic, minced
6 ounces Chinese sausages, diagonally cut into ¼-inch-thick slices
½ cup sliced bamboo shoots (½ of 8-ounce can), drained
1½ cups long-grain rice
2¾ cups water
3 green onions, thinly sliced

1. Place mushrooms in medium bowl and cover with hot water. Let stand 30 minutes. Drain and squeeze out excess water. Cut off and discard stems; cut caps into quarters.

2. For marinade, combine soy sauce, sherry, cornstarch, sugar, white pepper and 1 teaspoon of the ginger in large bowl; mix well. Add chicken and stir to coat well. Let stand 30 minutes.

Chicken and Chinese Sausages in Clay Pot

3. Drain chicken, reserving marinade. Heat oil in wok or large skillet over medium high heat. Add garlic and remaining 1 teaspoon ginger; stir-fry 30 seconds. Add chicken; stir-fry until browned, 2 to 3 minutes. Add mushrooms, Chinese sausages, bamboo shoots and reserved marinade. Stir-fry until chicken begins to turn opaque, about 4 minutes. Set aside.

4. Place rice in 3-quart clay pot or saucepan. Add water. Bring to a boil and cook, uncovered, over medium-high heat until crater-like holes form on surface, about 10 minutes.

5. Arrange chicken-sausage mixture on top of rice. Cover and steam over low heat until rice is tender and all liquid is absorbed, about 25 minutes. Sprinkle with onions; serve directly from clay pot.   *Makes 4 to 6 servings*

Chicken with Mangoes

1 cup all-purpose flour
1¾ cups water, divided
½ teaspoon salt
¼ teaspoon baking powder
3 whole boneless, skinless
    chicken breasts, cut into thin
    strips
  Vegetable oil for frying
1 piece fresh ginger (2×1 inch),
    pared and thinly sliced
3 tablespoons distilled white
    vinegar
3 tablespoons dry sherry

4 teaspoons soy sauce
2 teaspoons sugar
2 teaspoons cornstarch
2 teaspoons instant chicken
    bouillon granules
1 teaspoon sesame oil
8 green onions, cut into ½-inch
    pieces
1 can (15 ounces) mangoes,
    drained and cut into ½-inch
    strips
  Vermicelli (page 92), cooked
    and drained, optional

1. Combine flour, 1 cup of the water, the salt and baking powder in medium bowl. Beat with whisk until blended. Let stand 15 minutes. Add chicken; stir to coat well.

2. Heat vegetable oil in wok or large skillet to 375°F. Add chicken, one strip at a time (cook only about ¼ of the chicken strips at a time), and cook until golden, 3 to 5 minutes. Drain on paper towels. Repeat with remaining chicken.

3. Remove all but 1 tablespoon oil from wok. Reduce heat to medium. Add ginger; stir-fry until light brown, about 2 minutes.

4. Combine remaining ¾ cup water, the vinegar, sherry, soy sauce, sugar, cornstarch, bouillon granules and sesame oil in small bowl. Slowly pour into wok. Cook and stir until sauce boils. Add onions, reduce heat and simmer 3 minutes. Stir chicken and mangoes into wok. Cook and stir 2 minutes. Serve with Vermicelli, if desired.   *Makes 4 to 6 servings*

Chicken with Lychees

3 whole boneless, skinless
    chicken breasts
¼ cup plus 1 teaspoon
    cornstarch, divided
3 tablespoons vegetable oil
6 green onions, cut into 1-inch
    pieces
1 red bell pepper, cut into 1-inch
    pieces

½ cup tomato sauce
½ cup water, divided
1 teaspoon sugar
1 teaspoon instant chicken
    bouillon granules
1 can (11 ounces) whole peeled
    lychees, drained
Vermicelli (page 92), cooked
    and drained, optional

1. Cut chicken breasts in half; cut each half into 6 pieces. Place ¼ cup of the cornstarch in large bowl. Add chicken pieces and toss to coat well.

2. Heat oil in wok or large skillet over high heat. Add chicken and stir-fry until chicken is light brown, 5 to 8 minutes. Add onions and red pepper; stir-fry 1 minute.

3. Combine tomato sauce, ¼ cup of the water, the sugar and bouillon granules in small bowl; mix well. Pour over chicken-vegetable mixture. Stir in lychees. Reduce heat, cover and cook until chicken is tender, about 5 minutes.

4. Blend remaining ¼ cup water and 1 teaspoon cornstarch in small cup. Stir into chicken mixture. Cook and stir until sauce boils and thickens. Serve with Vermicelli, if desired.

Makes 4 servings

Chicken Chow Mein

Fried Noodles (page 92)
2½ tablespoons dry sherry, divided
2 tablespoons soy sauce, divided
3 teaspoons cornstarch, divided
2 whole boneless, skinless
    chicken breasts, cut into
    1-inch pieces
8 ounces boneless lean pork, cut
    into 1-inch pieces
½ cup water
2 teaspoons instant chicken
    bouillon granules
2 tablespoons vegetable oil
1 piece fresh ginger (1 inch
    square), pared and finely
    chopped

1 clove garlic, crushed
8 ounces shelled, deveined
    shrimp
2 medium yellow onions,
    chopped
1 red or green bell pepper, thinly
    sliced
2 stalks celery, diagonally cut
    into 1-inch slices
8 green onions, chopped
4 ounces cabbage (¼ of small
    head), shredded

Chicken Chow Mein

1. Prepare Fried Noodles; set aside.

2. Blend ½ tablespoon of the sherry, ½ tablespoon of the soy sauce and 1 teaspoon of the cornstarch in large bowl. Add chicken and pork; toss to coat well. Cover and refrigerate 1 hour.

3. Combine water, bouillon granules, remaining 2 teaspoons cornstarch, 2 tablespoons sherry and 1½ tablespoons soy sauce in small bowl; set aside. Heat oil in wok or large skillet over high heat. Add ginger and garlic and stir-fry 1 minute. Add chicken and pork; stir-fry until pork is no longer pink, about 5 minutes. Add shrimp; stir-fry until shrimp turn pink, about 3 minutes.

4. Add all vegetables to wok. Stir-fry until vegetables are crisp-tender, 3 to 5 minutes. Add bouillon-soy sauce mixture to wok. Cook and stir until sauce boils and thickens, then cook and stir 1 minute more.

5. Arrange Fried Noodles on serving plate; spoon chow mein over noodles.

Makes 6 servings

Asparagus Chicken with Black Bean Sauce

Asparagus Chicken with Black Bean Sauce

1 tablespoon dry sherry
4 teaspoons soy sauce, divided
5 teaspoons cornstarch, divided
1 teaspoon sesame oil
3 boneless, skinless chicken breast halves, cut into bite-size pieces
1 tablespoon fermented, salted black beans
1 teaspoon minced fresh ginger
1 clove garlic, minced

½ cup chicken broth
1 tablespoon oyster sauce
3 tablespoons vegetable oil, divided
1 pound fresh asparagus spears, trimmed and diagonally cut into 1-inch pieces
1 medium yellow onion, cut into 8 wedges and separated
2 tablespoons water

1. For marinade, combine sherry, 2 teaspoons of the soy sauce, 2 teaspoons of the cornstarch and the sesame oil in large bowl; mix well. Add chicken and stir to coat well. Let stand 30 minutes.

2. Place black beans in sieve and rinse under cold running water. Coarsely chop beans. Combine beans, ginger and garlic; finely chop all three together. Combine chicken broth, remaining 2 teaspoons soy sauce, the oyster sauce and the remaining 3 teaspoons cornstarch in small bowl; mix well and set aside.

3. Heat 2 tablespoons of the vegetable oil in wok or large skillet over high heat. Add chicken and stir-fry until chicken turns opaque, about 3 minutes. Remove and set aside.

4. Heat remaining 1 tablespoon vegetable oil in wok. Add asparagus and onion and stir-fry 30 seconds. Add water; cover and cook, stirring occasionally, until asparagus is crisp-tender, about 2 minutes. Return chicken to wok.

5. Stir chicken broth mixture and add to wok; cook and stir until sauce boils and thickens. *Makes 3 to 4 servings*

Honeyed Chicken and Pineapple

1 broiler/fryer chicken
   (3 to 4 pounds)
½ cup plus 2 teaspoons
   cornstarch, divided
   Vegetable oil for frying
2 teaspoons minced fresh ginger
1 clove garlic, crushed
1 can (20 ounces) pineapple
   chunks, drained

1 red or green bell pepper, thinly
   sliced
1½ cups water
1½ tablespoons honey
1 tablespoon instant chicken
   bouillon granules
1 teaspoon sesame oil
4 green onions, thinly sliced

1. Rinse chicken and cut into small serving-size pieces (see page 51). Place ½ cup of the cornstarch in large bowl. Add chicken pieces and toss to coat well.

2. Heat oil in wok or large skillet over high heat to 375°F. Add chicken pieces, one at a time (cook only ⅓ of the pieces at a time), and cook until golden and cooked through, about 5 minutes. Drain on paper towels. Repeat with remaining chicken.

3. Remove all but 2 tablespoons oil from wok. Add ginger and garlic and stir-fry 1 minute. Add pineapple and red pepper; stir-fry 2 minutes. Remove and set aside.

4. Combine water and remaining 2 teaspoons cornstarch in small bowl. Blend in honey, bouillon granules and sesame oil. Pour mixture into wok; cook and stir until sauce boils and thickens. Return chicken and pineapple-pepper mixture to wok; cook and stir until heated through. Add green onions; cook and stir 1 minute more. *Makes 4 servings*

Chicken with Water Chestnuts

1 ounce dried mushrooms
⅔ cup water
4 teaspoons cornstarch
1 tablespoon instant chicken
  bouillon granules
1 tablespoon dry sherry
1 tablespoon soy sauce
1 tablespoon oyster sauce
1½ cups vegetable oil
2 whole boneless, skinless
  chicken breasts, cut into
  1-inch pieces

3 stalks celery, diagonally cut
  into ½-inch slices
1 red or green bell pepper, thinly
  sliced
1 medium yellow onion, cut into
  wedges and separated
1 can (8 ounces) water chestnuts,
  drained and cut into halves
8 ounces bean sprouts
1 piece (about 1 inch square)
  fresh ginger, pared and
  thinly sliced

1. Place mushrooms in medium bowl and cover with hot water. Let stand 30 minutes. Drain and squeeze out excess water. Remove and discard stems; cut caps into halves.

2. Combine water, cornstarch, bouillon granules, sherry, soy sauce and oyster sauce in small bowl; mix well.

3. Heat oil in wok or large skillet over high heat to 375°F. Add chicken pieces, one at a time (cook only ½ of the pieces at a time), and cook until golden, about 5 minutes. Drain on paper towels.

4. Remove all but 2 tablespoons oil from wok. Add mushrooms, celery, red pepper, onion, water chestnuts. bean sprouts, ginger and chicken to wok. Toss to mix well.

5. Stir water mixture and add to wok. Cook and stir until vegetables are crisp-tender, 3 to 5 minutes.   *Makes 4 servings*

Ginger Green Onion Chicken

1 broiler/fryer chicken
  (3 to 4 pounds)
1 piece fresh ginger (2×1-inch),
  pared and thinly sliced
1¼ teaspoons salt, divided
½ teaspoon pepper, divided
⅓ cup vegetable oil
8 green onions, finely chopped

3 tablespoons minced fresh
  ginger
2 teaspoons distilled white
  vinegar
1 teaspoon soy sauce
  Steamed Rice (page 90),
  optional

Ginger Green Onion Chicken

1. Rinse chicken and place in large stockpot or Dutch oven. Add sliced ginger, 1 teaspoon of the salt, ¼ teaspoon of the pepper and enough water to cover chicken. Cover and bring to a boil over high heat. Reduce heat and simmer until tender, about 40 minutes. Let stand until cool.

2. Strain stock and refrigerate or freeze for another use. Refrigerate chicken until cold, then cut into small serving-size pieces (see page 51).

3. Combine remaining ¼ teaspoon salt, ¼ teaspoon pepper, oil, onions, ginger, vinegar and soy sauce in jar with tight-fitting lid. Shake to mix well. Refrigerate 1 to 2 hours.

4. Place chicken in serving bowl. Shake onion-ginger mixture and pour over chicken. Serve with Steamed Rice, if desired.   *Makes 4 to 6 servings*

Fish & Seafood

Clams in Black Bean Sauce

24 small hard-shell clams
1½ tablespoons fermented, salted black beans
2 cloves garlic, minced
1 teaspoon minced fresh ginger
2 tablespoons vegetable oil
2 green onions, thinly sliced
1 cup chicken broth

2 tablespoons dry sherry
1 tablespoon soy sauce
1½ to 2 cups Chinese-style thin egg noodles, cooked and drained
3 tablespoons chopped cilantro (Chinese parsley) or parsley, for garnish

1. Scrub clams under cold running water with stiff brush. (Discard any shells that refuse to close when tapped.)

2. Place black beans in sieve and rinse under cold running water. Coarsely chop beans. Combine beans with garlic and ginger; finely chop all three together.

3. Heat oil in 5-quart pot over medium heat. Add black bean mixture and onions; stir-fry 30 seconds. Add clams and stir to coat.

4. Add chicken broth, sherry and soy sauce to pot. Bring to a boil; reduce heat, cover and simmer until clam shells open, 5 to 8 minutes. (Discard any clams that do not open.)

5. To serve, divide noodles equally among 4 large bowls. Arrange clams on top. Ladle broth over clams. Garnish each serving with chopped cilantro.

Makes 4 servings

Clams in Black Bean Sauce

Braised Trout with Sweet and Pungent Sauce

Braised Trout with Sweet and Pungent Sauce

½ cup chicken broth
¼ cup sugar
¼ cup distilled white vinegar
1 tablespoon catsup
1½ teaspoons soy sauce
4 whole cleaned trout
(about 8 ounces each)
Salt and pepper
¼ cup plus 2 teaspoons
cornstarch, divided
3 tablespoons vegetable oil,
divided

2 thin slices pared fresh ginger,
cut into thin shreds
½ small carrot, shredded
¼ cup sliced bamboo shoots
(¼ of 8-ounce can),
shredded
¼ cup Chinese mixed pickled
vegetables (¼ of 12-ounce
jar), sliced
2 green onions, cut into 2-inch
slivers
1 tablespoon water

1. For sauce, combine chicken broth, sugar, vinegar, catsup and soy sauce in small bowl; mix well.

2. Sprinkle fish lightly with salt and pepper. Lightly coat using ¼ cup of the cornstarch; shake off excess.

3. Heat 2 tablespoons of the oil in large nonstick skillet over medium-high heat. Add fish and cook until lightly browned, about 2 minutes on each side. Remove and set aside.

4. Discard drippings from skillet and wipe clean with paper towels. Heat remaining 1 tablespoon oil in skillet. Add ginger and stir-fry 10 seconds. Add carrot and bamboo shoots; stir-fry 30 seconds. Return fish to wok. Add pickled vegetables and onions. Pour in chicken broth mixture. Cover and simmer until fish turns opaque and flakes easily with fork, about 3 minutes.

5. While fish is cooking, blend remaining 2 teaspoons cornstarch and the water in small cup. Using slotted spoon, transfer fish to serving platter. Pour cornstarch mixture into wok. Cook and stir until sauce boils and thickens. Spoon sauce over fish.

Makes 4 servings

Seafood Combination

Fried Noodles (see page 92)
4 tablespoons vegetable oil, divided
8 green onions, diagonally cut into thin slices
3 stalks celery, diagonally cut into thin slices
1 can (8 ounces) water chestnuts, drained and cut into halves
1 can (8 ounces) bamboo shoots, thinly sliced
8 ounces fresh or thawed frozen sea scallops, cut into quarters
8 ounces fresh or thawed frozen shrimp, shelled and deveined
8 ounces fresh or thawed frozen fish fillets, skinned and cut into 1½-inch square pieces
8 ounces cleaned, ready-to-cook squid, optional
½ cup water
1 tablespoon soy sauce
2 teaspoons dry sherry
2 teaspoons cornstarch
1 teaspoon instant chicken bouillon granules

1. Prepare Fried Noodles; set aside.

2. Heat 2 tablespoons of the oil in wok or large skillet over high heat. Add onions, celery, water chestnuts and bamboo shoots; stir-fry until crisp-tender, about 2 minutes. Remove and set aside.

3. Heat remaining 2 tablespoons oil in wok over high heat. Add scallops, shrimp, fish pieces and squid; stir-fry until all fish turns opaque and is cooked through, about 3 minutes.

4. Combine water, soy sauce, sherry, cornstarch and bouillon granules in small bowl. Add to wok. Cook and stir until liquid boils. Return vegetables to wok; cook and stir 2 minutes more. Serve with Fried Noodles.

Makes 6 servings

Crab-Stuffed Shrimp

SAUCE

- 2 tablespoons vegetable oil
- 1 small yellow onion, finely chopped
- 1 teaspoon curry powder
- 1½ tablespoons dry sherry
- 1 tablespoon satay sauce
- 1 teaspoon sugar
- 2 teaspoons soy sauce
- ¼ cup cream or milk

SHRIMP

- 2 egg whites
- 4 teaspoons cornstarch
- 1 tablespoon dry sherry
- 1 tablespoon soy sauce
- 2 cans (6½ ounces each) crab meat, drained and flaked
- 8 green onions, finely chopped
- 2 stalks celery, finely chopped
- 1½ pounds large shrimp, shelled and deveined
- ½ cup all-purpose flour
- 3 eggs
- 3 tablespoons milk
- 2 to 3 cups soft bread crumbs (8 to 10 bread slices)
- Vegetable oil for frying

1. For sauce, heat 2 tablespoons oil in small saucepan over medium heat. Add onion and cook until onion is transparent, about 3 minutes. Add curry powder; cook and stir 1 minute. Add sherry, satay sauce, sugar and soy sauce; cook and stir 2 minutes. Stir in cream; bring to a boil. Boil 2 minutes. Keep warm.

2. For shrimp, blend egg whites, cornstarch, sherry and soy sauce in medium bowl. Add crab meat, onions and celery; mix well.

3. Cut deep slit into but not through back of each shrimp. Flatten shrimp by pounding gently with mallet or rolling pin. Spoon crab mixture onto each shrimp and press with back of spoon or small spatula.

4. Coat each shrimp lightly with flour. Beat eggs and milk with fork in shallow bowl until blended. Place each shrimp stuffed-side up in egg mixture, then spoon mixture over shrimp to cover completely. Coat each shrimp completely with bread crumbs, pressing crumbs lightly onto shrimp. Place shrimp in single layer on cookie sheets or plates. Refrigerate 30 minutes.

5. Heat oil in wok or large skillet over high heat to 375°F. Cook 4 or 5 shrimp at a time until golden, about 3 minutes. Drain on paper towels. Serve with warm sauce.

Makes 4 servings

Braised Shrimp with Vegetables

Braised Shrimp with Vegetables

1 tablespoon vegetable oil
1 pound large shrimp, shelled
   and deveined
8 ounces fresh broccoli, cut into
   small pieces
2 cans (4 ounces each) whole
   button mushrooms, drained
1 can (8 ounces) bamboo shoots,
   thinly sliced

½ cup chicken broth
1 teaspoon cornstarch
1 teaspoon oyster sauce
¼ teaspoon sugar
½ teaspoon minced fresh ginger
⅛ teaspoon pepper

1. Heat oil in wok or large skillet over high heat. Add shrimp and stir-fry until shrimp turn pink, about 3 minutes.

2. Add broccoli to wok; stir-fry 1 minute. Add mushrooms and bamboo shoots; stir-fry 1 minute more.

3. Combine remaining ingredients in small bowl; mix well. Pour over shrimp-vegetable mixture. Cook and stir until sauce boils and thickens, about 2 minutes more. *Makes 4 servings*

Chinese Steamed Fish

1 fresh whole fish
(about 2 pounds), such as
rock cod, red snapper or
kingfish; or 1 pound fish
fillets or steaks, such as sea
bass, ling cod, halibut or red
snapper
1 to 2 teaspoons salt

5 green onions
1 piece fresh ginger (about
2×1½ inches), pared and cut
into 1½-inch slivers
2 tablespoons vegetable oil
2 tablespoons soy sauce
Cilantro sprigs (Chinese
parsley), for garnish

1. If using whole fish, clean and scale. Make 3 diagonal slashes on each side. Rub fish with 2 teaspoons salt. (If using fillets, rub with 1 teaspoon salt.) Cut 2 of the green onions into 2-inch pieces. Cut the remaining 3 onions into 1½-inch slivers.

2. Place onion pieces in a rimmed heatproof dish that will fit inside a steamer. Place whole fish on top (or place fillets in single layer on top). Place ½ of ginger and ½ of onion slivers on top of fish.

3. Place dish on rack in steamer. Cover and steam over boiling water until fish turns opaque and flakes easily with fork. Steam about 10 minutes per inch of thickness. While fish is cooking, heat oil in small pan until very hot but not smoking.

4. Remove dish from steamer. Pour off about ½ of pan juices. Pour soy sauce over fish. Sprinkle with remaining ginger and onion slivers. Carefully pour hot oil over fish (oil will sizzle.) Garnish with cilantro sprigs.

Makes 4 to 6 servings

Chinese Steamed Fish

Butterfly Shrimp

1½ pounds large shrimp, shelled
    and deveined, leaving tails
    intact
  3 egg yolks
1½ teaspoons cornstarch

½ teaspoon salt
⅛ teaspoon pepper
2 slices bacon, cut into
    1½×¼-inch strips
  Vegetable oil for frying

1. Cut deep slit down back of each shrimp. Flatten cut side slightly with fingers.

2. Beat egg yolks, cornstarch, salt and pepper with fork in medium bowl. Dip each shrimp into egg mixture. Place a bacon strip on cut side of each shrimp.

3. Heat oil in wok or large skillet over medium-high heat to 400°F. Cook shrimp, a few at a time, until golden, 2 to 3 minutes. Drain on paper towels.

Makes 4 to 6 main dish or 8 to 10 appetizer servings

Fish Rolls with Crab Sauce

FISH ROLLS

1 pound sole fillets, ¼- to
    ⅜-inch thick each
    (about 4 ounces each)
1 tablespoon dry sherry
2 teaspoons sesame oil

1 green onion, minced
1 teaspoon minced fresh ginger
½ teaspoon salt
  Dash ground white pepper

CRAB SAUCE

1½ tablespoons cornstarch
  2 tablespoons water
  1 tablespoon vegetable oil
  1 teaspoon minced fresh ginger
  2 green onions, thinly sliced

1 tablespoon dry sherry
6 ounces fresh crab meat, flaked
1¼ cups chicken broth
¼ cup milk

1. For fish rolls, if fillets are large, cut in half crosswise (each piece should be 5 to 6 inches long). Combine sherry, sesame oil, minced onion, ginger, salt and white pepper in small bowl. Brush each piece of fish with marinade. Let stand 30 minutes.

2. Roll fillets into small bundles. Place on rimmed heatproof dish that will fit inside a steamer. Place dish on rack in steamer. Cover and steam over boiling water until fish turns opaque and flakes easily with fork, 8 to 10 minutes.

Fish Rolls with Crab Sauce

3. For crab sauce, blend cornstarch and water in small cup. Heat oil in 2-quart saucepan over medium heat. Add ginger and cook 10 seconds. Add sliced onions, sherry and crab meat; stir-fry 1 minute. Add chicken broth and milk; bring to a simmer. Stir cornstarch mixture and add to saucepan; cook, stirring, until sauce boils and thickens slightly.

4. Using slotted spoon, transfer fish to serving platter. Pour crab sauce over fish.   *Makes 4 to 6 servings*

Fragrant Braised Oysters

Fragrant Braised Oysters

1 jar (10 or 12 ounces) shucked
    oysters, drained
2 cups plus 1 tablespoon water,
    divided
½ teaspoon salt
¼ cup chicken broth
1 tablespoon dry sherry
1 tablespoon oyster sauce
1 teaspoon cornstarch
¼ teaspoon sugar

2 tablespoons vegetable oil,
    divided
3 slices (about ½-inch each)
    pared fresh ginger, cut into
    thin slivers
½ small yellow onion, cut into
    wedges and separated
3 green onions, cut into 2-inch
    pieces

1. If oysters are large, cut into bite-size pieces. In 2-quart saucepan, bring 2 cups of the water and the salt to a boil. Add oysters. Turn off heat and let stand 30 seconds. Drain, rinse under cold running water and drain again.

2. Combine chicken broth, sherry, oyster sauce, remaining 1 tablespoon water, the cornstarch and sugar in small bowl; mix well.

3. Heat 1 tablespoon of the oil in wok or large skillet over high heat. Add ginger and yellow onion; stir-fry 1 minute. Add green onions; stir-fry 30 seconds. Remove and set aside.

4. Heat remaining 1 tablespoon oil in wok. Add blanched oysters and stir-fry 2 minutes. Return ginger and onions to wok. Stir cornstarch mixture and add to wok. Cook and stir until sauce boils and thickens.   *Makes 2 to 3 servings*

Shrimp Omelets

3 to 5 tablespoons vegetable oil,
    divided
8 fresh medium mushrooms,
    finely chopped
1 cup water
4 teaspoons cornstarch
1 teaspoon sugar
2 teaspoons soy sauce
2 teaspoons instant chicken
    bouillon granules
8 eggs
½ teaspoon salt
⅛ teaspoon pepper
8 ounces bean sprouts
8 ounces shrimp, shelled,
    deveined and finely chopped
4 green onions, finely chopped
1 stalk celery, finely chopped
2 green onions, thinly sliced

1. Heat 1 tablespoon of the oil in small skillet. Add mushrooms and cook 1 minute. Remove and set aside.

2. Combine water, cornstarch, sugar, soy sauce and bouillon granules in small saucepan. Cook over medium heat until mixture boils and thickens, about 5 minutes. Keep warm.

3. Combine eggs, salt and pepper in large bowl. Beat until frothy. Add sprouts, shrimp, chopped onions, celery and mushrooms; mix well.

4. For each omelet, heat ½ tablespoon oil in 7-inch omelet pan or skillet. Pour ½ cup egg mixture into pan. Cook until light brown, 2 to 3 minutes on each side. Stack omelets on serving plate. Pour warm soy sauce mixture over omelets. Garnish with sliced onions.   *Makes 4 servings*

Crab in Ginger Sauce

2 ready-to-cook, whole hard-shell crabs
¾ cup water, divided
2½ tablespoons dry sherry
1 teaspoon sugar
1 teaspoon instant chicken bouillon granules
2 teaspoons soy sauce
2 teaspoons cornstarch

2 tablespoons vegetable oil
½ teaspoon sesame oil
1 piece (about 4×1 inches) fresh ginger, pared and cut into thin strips
1 red bell pepper, cut into thin strips
8 green onions, cut into 1-inch pieces

1. Rinse crabs under cold running water. Gently pull away round hard shell on top. With small sharp knife, gently cut away the gray spongy tissue and discard. Rinse again under cold running water.

2. Cut off claws and legs. Pound claws lightly with back of cleaver or hammer to break shells. Chop down center of crab to cut body in half. Cut each half crosswise into 3 pieces.

3. Combine ½ cup of the water, the sherry, sugar, bouillon granules and soy sauce in small bowl; mix well. Blend remaining ¼ cup water and the cornstarch in small cup.

4. Heat vegetable and sesame oils in wok or large skillet over medium heat. Add ginger and stir-fry 1 minute. Add crab pieces; stir-fry 1 minute.

5. Add sherry mixture and red pepper to wok; stir-fry over high heat until liquid boils. Reduce heat, cover and simmer 4 minutes. Stir cornstarch mixture and add to wok. Cook and stir until sauce boils and thickens. Add onions; cook and stir 1 minute more. *Makes 4 to 6 servings*

Scallops with Vegetables

1 ounce dried mushrooms
2 tablespoons vegetable oil
2 yellow onions, cut into wedges and separated
3 stalks celery, diagonally cut into ½-inch pieces
8 ounces fresh green beans, trimmed and diagonally cut into 1-inch pieces
2 teaspoons minced fresh ginger
1 clove garlic, minced
1 cup water

2½ tablespoons dry sherry
4 teaspoons soy sauce
4 teaspoons cornstarch
2 teaspoons instant chicken bouillon granules
1 pound fresh of thawed frozen sea scallops, cut into quarters
6 green onions, diagonally cut into thin slices
1 can (15 ounces) baby corn, drained

Scallops with Vegetables

1. Place mushrooms in bowl and cover with hot water. Let stand 30 minutes. Drain and squeeze out excess water. Cut off and discard stems; cut caps into thin slices.

2. Heat oil in wok or large skillet over high heat. Add yellow onions, celery, green beans, ginger and garlic; stir-fry 3 minutes.

3. Combine water, sherry, soy sauce, cornstarch and bouillon granules in small bowl. Add to wok. Cook and stir until sauce boils.

4. Add scallops, mushrooms, green onions and baby corn. Cook and stir until scallops turn opaque, about 4 minutes.   *Makes 4 to 6 servings*

Vegetable Dishes

Zucchini Shanghai Style

4 dried mushrooms
½ cup chicken broth
2 tablespoons catsup
2 teaspoons soy sauce
1 teaspoon dry sherry
¼ teaspoon sugar
⅛ teaspoon salt
1 teaspoon red wine vinegar
2 tablespoons vegetable oil, divided
1 teaspoon minced fresh ginger

1 clove garlic, minced
1 green onion, minced
1 large tomato, peeled, seeded and chopped
4 tablespoons water, divided
1 teaspoon cornstarch
1 pound zucchini, diagonally cut into 1-inch pieces
½ small yellow onion, cut into wedges and separated

1. Place mushrooms in bowl and cover with hot water. Let stand 30 minutes. Drain, reserving ¼ cup liquid. Squeeze out excess water. Cut off and discard stems; cut caps into thin slices.

2. Combine the reserved ¼ cup mushroom liquid, the chicken broth, catsup, soy sauce, sherry, sugar, salt and vinegar in small bowl.

3. Heat 1 tablespoon of the oil in 2-quart saucepan over medium-high heat. Add ginger and garlic and stir-fry 10 seconds. Add mushrooms, green onion and tomato. Stir-fry 1 minute. Add chicken broth mixture and bring to a boil; reduce heat and simmer, uncovered, 10 minutes.

Zucchini Shanghai Style

4. Blend 1 tablespoon of the water and the cornstarch in small cup. Heat remaining 1 tablespoon oil in wok or large skillet over medium-high heat. Add zucchini and yellow onion and stir-fry 30 seconds. Add remaining 2 tablespoons water, cover and cook, stirring occasionally, until vegetables are crisp-tender, 3 to 4 minutes.

5. Pour tomato sauce into wok. Stir cornstarch mixture and add to wok. Cook and stir until sauce boils and thickens.   *Makes 4 to 6 servings*

Eggplant Szechuan Style

Eggplant Szechuan Style

1 pound Oriental eggplants or
    1 domestic eggplant
3 green onions
1 tablespoon minced garlic
2 teaspoons minced fresh ginger
2 teaspoons hot bean sauce
½ cup chicken broth
1 tablespoon soy sauce

1 tablespoon red wine vinegar
1½ teaspoons sugar
5 tablespoons vegetable oil,
    divided
1 tablespoon water
1 teaspoon cornstarch
1 teaspoon sesame oil

1. Cut unpeeled eggplant into ½-inch thick slices; cut slices into 2×½-inch strips.

2. Cut 1 of the green onions into thin slices; reserve for garnish. Cut remaining 2 green onions into thin slices. Combine onions, garlic, ginger and hot bean sauce in medium bowl. Combine chicken broth, soy sauce, vinegar and sugar in small bowl.

3. Heat 2 tablespoons of the vegetable oil in wok or large skillet over medium-high heat. Add ½ of eggplant and cook, stirring often, until soft and moist, about 5 minutes. Remove to a colander to drain. Repeat, using 2 more tablespoons vegetable oil and the remaining eggplant.

4. Heat remaining 1 tablespoon vegetable oil in wok over medium-high heat. Add onion-garlic mixture and stir-fry 30 seconds, Return eggplant to wok. Add chicken broth mixture. Bring to a boil and cook, stirring occasionally, until liquid is almost evaporated.

5. Blend water and cornstarch in small cup; add to wok. Cook and stir until sauce boils and thickens slightly. Stir in sesame oil. Garnish with reserved onion slices. *Makes 4 to 5 servings*

Chinese Vegetables

1 pound fresh broccoli
¾ cup water
1 tablespoon instant chicken bouillon granules
2 tablespoons vegetable oil
2 medium yellow onions, cut into wedges and separated
1 tablespoon minced fresh ginger
8 ounces fresh spinach, coarsely chopped

8 ounces fresh snow peas or 1 package (6 ounces) thawed frozen snow peas, trimmed and strings removed
4 stalks celery, diagonally cut into ½-inch pieces
8 green onions, diagonally cut into thin slices

1. Cut broccoli tops into florets. Cut stalks into 2×¼-inch thin strips. Combine water and bouillon granules in small bowl; mix well.

2. Heat oil in wok or large skillet over high heat. Add broccoli stalks, yellow onions and ginger; stir-fry 1 minute. Add all remaining vegetables; toss lightly.

3. Add water mixture. Toss until vegetables well coated. Bring to a boil, cover and cook until vegetables are crisp-tender, 2 to 3 minutes.
Makes 4 to 6 servings

NOTE: Sliced carrots, zucchini, green beans or green bell peppers may be used in addition to, or in place of, the listed vegetables.

Quick Stir-Fried Vegetables

2 cups cauliflower florets
  (about ½ of small head)
3 cups broccoli florets
  (about 1 pound broccoli)
½ small jicama (about 8 ounces),
  pared
2 tablespoons vegetable oil

1 teaspoon minced fresh ginger
½ cup chicken broth, divided
¼ teaspoon salt
¼ teaspoon sugar
1 red bell pepper, cut into thin
  strips
1 teaspoon sesame oil

1. Cut a small x in stem end of each cauliflower floret. If florets are large, cut them into 2 or 3 slices. Cut a small x in stem end of broccoli florets. Cut jicama into thick slices, then cut into 2×¼-inch strips. Set all vegetables, oil and seasonings near cooking area.

2. Heat vegetable oil in wok or large skillet over high heat. Add ginger and stir-fry 10 seconds. Add cauliflower and broccoli; stir-fry 30 seconds to coat with oil.

3. Pour about ⅓ cup of the chicken broth around edges of wok. Add salt and sugar. Cover and cook until vegetables are partially tender, 3 to 4 minutes.

4. Add jicama, bell pepper and remaining chicken broth. Cover and cook 1 minute. Uncover and stir-fry until vegetables are crisp-tender and all liquid has evaporated. Stir in sesame oil. *Makes 4 to 6 servings*

Bean Curd with Oyster Sauce

2 tablespoons vegetable oil,
  divided
8 ounces bean curd, cut into
  ½-inch cubes
½ cup water
2 tablespoons oyster sauce
1 tablespoon cornstarch
4 teaspoons dry sherry

4 teaspoons soy sauce
4 ounces fresh mushrooms, sliced
6 green onions, cut into 1-inch
  pieces
3 stalks celery, diagonally cut
  into ½-inch pieces
1 red or green bell pepper, cut
  into ½-inch chunks

1. Heat 1 tablespoon of the oil in wok or large skillet over high heat. Add bean curd and stir-fry until light brown, about 3 minutes. Remove and set aside. Combine water, oyster sauce, cornstarch, sherry and soy sauce in small bowl.

2. Heat remaining 1 tablespoon oil in wok over high heat. Add all vegetables; stir-fry 1 minute.

3. Return bean curd to wok; toss lightly to combine. Add cornstarch-soy mixture to wok. Cook and stir until liquid boils; cook 1 minute more. *Makes 4 servings*

Quick Stir-Fried Vegetables

Chinese Mixed Pickled Vegetables

PICKLING LIQUID

3 cups sugar
3 cups distilled white vinegar

1½ cups water
1½ teaspoons salt

VEGETABLES

3 large carrots, cut into 2-inch
  long thin strips
1 large Chinese white radish
  (about 1 pound), cut into
  2-inch long thin strips
1 large cucumber, seeded and cut
  into 2-inch long thin strips
4 stalks celery, diagonally cut
  into ½-inch pieces

8 green onions, diagonally cut
  into ¼-inch pieces
4 ounces fresh ginger, pared and
  thinly sliced
1 large red bell pepper, cut into
  ½-inch cubes
1 large green bell pepper, cut
  into ½-inch cubes

1. Combine all pickling liquid ingredients in 3-quart saucepan. Bring to a boil, stirring, over medium heat. Cool.

2. For vegetables, fill 5-quart stockpot or Dutch oven ½ full of water. Bring to a boil and add all vegetables. Remove from heat and let stand 2 minutes.

3. Drain vegetables in large colander. Spread vegetables out on clean towels; allow to dry 2 to 3 hours.

4. Pack vegetables firmly into clean jars with tight-fitting lids. Pour Pickling Liquid into jars to cover vegetables. Seal jars tightly. Store in refrigerator at least 1 week before using.   *Makes 1½ to 2 quarts*

Ma-Po Bean Curd

1 tablespoon Szechuan
  peppercorns, optional
¾ cup chicken broth
1 tablespoon soy sauce
1 tablespoon dry sherry
2 tablespoons vegetable oil
4 ounces ground pork
2 teaspoons minced fresh ginger
2 cloves garlic, minced

1 tablespoon hot bean sauce
12 to 14 ounces bean curd,
  drained and cut into ½-inch
  cubes
2 green onions, thinly sliced
3 tablespoons water
1½ tablespoons cornstarch
1 teaspoon sesame oil

1. Place peppercorns in small dry skillet; shake over medium-low heat, until fragrant, about 2 minutes. Let cool. Crush peppercorns with mortar and pestle or place between paper towels and crush with hammer.*

*Note: Szechuan peppercorns are deceptively potent. Wear rubber or plastic gloves when crushing them and do not touch eyes or lips when handling.

Ma-Po Bean Curd

2. Combine chicken broth, soy sauce and sherry in small bowl.

3. Heat vegetable oil in wok or large skillet over high heat. Add pork and stir-fry until pork is no longer pink, about 2 minutes. Add ginger, garlic and hot bean sauce. Stir-fry until meat absorbs color from bean sauce, about 1 minute.

4. Add chicken broth mixture and bean curd to wok. Simmer, uncovered, 5 minutes. Stir in onions. Blend water and cornstarch in small cup. Add to wok; cook and stir until sauce boils and thickens slightly. Stir in sesame oil. Pass ground peppercorns separately to sprinkle over each serving, if desired.

Makes 3 to 4 servings

Shrimp-Stuffed Bean Curd

SHRIMP STUFFING

4 ounces shrimp, shelled,
  deveined and finely chopped
2 tablespoons minced water
  chestnuts
2 teaspoons minced green onions

1 teaspoon dry sherry
1 teaspoon cornstarch
¼ teaspoon salt
½ teaspoon sesame oil

BEAN CURD

1 package (about 1 pound) bean
  curd
3 tablespoons vegetable oil,
  divided
1 cup chicken broth
1 tablespoon soy sauce
½ teaspoon sugar

½ teaspoon fresh ginger
½ small head napa cabbage, cut
  into 2-inch squares
½ cup straw mushrooms
¼ cup thawed frozen peas
1 tablespoon cornstarch
1 tablespoon water

1. Combine all shrimp stuffing ingredients in medium bowl; mix well.

2. Drain bean curd. Cut bean curd crosswise through the middle to make 8
triangles. Place between paper towels and gently press out excess water.

Shrimp-Stuffed Bean Curd

3. Cut a pocket in longest side of each triangle. Scoop out ½-inch hole with spoon or knife. Fill hole with 1 tablespoon shrimp filling. Smooth top.

4. Heat 2 tablespoons of the oil in wok or large nonstick skillet over medium heat. Add stuffed bean curd triangles, flat-side down. Cook until golden brown, about 3 minutes on each side. Stand triangles in wok and cook filled-side down 30 seconds. Remove and set aside. Discard drippings; wipe wok clean with paper towels.

5. Combine chicken broth, soy sauce and sugar in small bowl. Heat remaining 1 tablespoon oil in wok over medium-high heat. Add ginger and stir-fry 10 seconds. Add cabbage; stir-fry until cabbage begins to wilt, about 2 minutes. Arrange bean curd triangles on top of cabbage. Sprinkle with straw mushrooms and peas.

6. Pour chicken broth mixture over bean curd. Cover and bring just to a boil; reduce heat and simmer 10 minutes. Blend cornstarch and water in small cup. Gently push bean curd to one side of wok; stir cornstarch mixture into liquid. Cook, stirring carefully, until sauce boils and thickens.   *Makes 4 servings*

Braised Choice Vegetables

8 dried mushrooms
1 can (15 ounces) peeled straw
   mushrooms
1 cup baby corn (½ of 15-ounce
   can)
½ cup sliced bamboo shoots
   (½ of 8-ounce can)

2 tablespoons oyster sauce
2 teaspoons soy sauce
2 tablespoons vegetable oil
1 clove garlic, minced
½ cup chicken broth
2 teaspoons cornstarch
1 tablespoon water

1. Place dried mushrooms in bowl and cover with hot water. Let stand 30 minutes. Drain, reserving ½ cup liquid. Squeeze out excess water. Cut off and discard stems. Leave mushrooms whole, or, if large, cut into halves.

2. Drain straw mushrooms, baby corn and bamboo shoots. If corn is large, diagonally cut each ear into small pieces. Rinse under cold running water and drain. Combine oyster sauce and soy sauce in small cup.

3. Heat oil in wok or large skillet over high heat. Add garlic and stir-fry 10 seconds. Add dried mushrooms; stir-fry 1 minute. Add chicken broth and reserved ½ cup mushroom liquid. Cover and simmer over medium heat until mushrooms are tender and about ½ the liquid has evaporated, about 5 minutes.

4. Add straw mushrooms, corn, bamboo shoots and soy sauce mixture. Simmer 3 minutes. Blend cornstarch and water in small cup. Stir into wok; cook and stir until sauce boils and thickens slightly.   *Makes 4 to 6 servings*

Rice & Noodles

Lo Mein Noodles with Shrimp

12 ounces Chinese-style thin egg noodles
2 teaspoons sesame oil
1½ tablespoons oyster sauce
1½ tablespoons soy sauce
½ teaspoon sugar
¼ teaspoon salt
¼ teaspoon ground white pepper
2 tablespoons vegetable oil
1 teaspoon minced fresh ginger

1 clove garlic, minced
8 ounces medium shrimp, shelled and deveined
1 tablespoon dry sherry
½ cup Chinese chives, cut into 1-inch pieces or ¼ cup domestic chives, cut into 1-inch pieces and 2 green onions, cut into 1-inch pieces
8 ounces bean sprouts

1. Cook noodles according to package directions until tender but still firm, 2 to 3 minutes. Drain, rinse under cold running water and drain again. Toss noodles with sesame oil until well coated.

2. Combine oyster sauce, soy sauce, sugar, salt and pepper in small bowl.

3. Heat vegetable oil in wok or large skillet over high heat. Add ginger and garlic and stir-fry 10 seconds. Add shrimp; stir-fry until shrimp begin to turn pink, about 1 minute. Add sherry and chives; stir-fry until chives begin to wilt, about 15 seconds. Add ½ of bean sprouts; stir-fry 15 seconds. Add remaining bean sprouts; stir-fry 15 seconds more.

4. Add oyster sauce mixture and noodles. Cook and stir until heated through, about 2 minutes. *Makes 4 servings*

Lo Mein Noodles with Shrimp

Noodle Baskets

~~~~~~

8 ounces Chinese-style thin egg noodles

Vegetable oil for frying

1. Cook noodles according to package directions until tender but still firm, 2 to 3 minutes. Drain, rinse under cold running water and drain again.

2. Place several layers of paper towels over cookie sheets or jelly-roll pans. Spread noodles over paper towels and let dry at least 8 hours or overnight.

3. Brush inside of medium strainer (about 5 inches in diameter) with a small amount of oil. Spread an even layer of noodles about ½ inch thick in strainer. Brush rounded outside of another strainer with oil. Place second strainer rounded-side down over noodles in first strainer. Press lightly.

4. Heat remaining oil in wok or deep saucepan over medium-high heat to 375°F. Carefully lower the two strainers, holding handles together, into hot oil. Cook until noodles are golden, 2 to 3 minutes. Remove from oil and place on paper towels. Carefully remove top and bottom strainers, running knife blade around edge of noodles if necessary to loosen noodle basket. Drain baskets on paper towels. Repeat with remaining noodles. *Makes 6 to 8 baskets*

Note: These noodle baskets can be used to serve Chinese food in an unusual and attractive way. To prepare in advance, cook as directed, wrap securely in plastic wrap and store in refrigerator up to three days or in freezer up to three weeks. To reheat, remove from plastic, arrange on cookie sheet, and bake in preheated 325°F oven until heated through, 8 to 10 minutes.

Vegetarian Fried Rice

~~~~~~

4 dried mushrooms
4 cups cooked long-grain rice
3 eggs
¾ teaspoon salt, divided
2½ tablespoons vegetable oil, divided
1 teaspoon minced fresh ginger
1 clove garlic, minced

3 green onions, thinly sliced
4 ounces bean curd, cut into ¼-inch cubes and deep fried
1 tablespoon soy sauce
¼ teaspoon sugar
1 cup bean sprouts, coarsely chopped
½ cup thawed frozen peas

1. Place mushrooms in small bowl and cover with hot water. Let stand 30 minutes. Drain, reserving liquid. Squeeze out excess water. Cut off and discard stems; dice caps.

2. Rub rice with wet hands so all the grains are separated.

3. Beat eggs with ¼ teaspoon of the salt in medium bowl. Heat ½ tablespoon oil in wok or large skillet over medium heat. Add eggs; cook and stir until soft curds form. Remove from heat and cut eggs into small pieces using a spoon. Remove and set aside.

Vegetarian Fried Rice

4. Heat remaining 2 tablespoons oil in wok over high heat. Add ginger, garlic and onions; stir-fry 10 seconds. Add mushrooms, ¼ cup of the reserved mushroom soaking liquid, the bean curd, soy sauce and sugar. Cook until most of the liquid evaporates, about 4 minutes. Add bean sprouts and peas; cook 30 seconds.

5. Add rice and remaining ½ teaspoon salt. Stir and toss until heated through. Add a few drops mushroom soaking liquid if rice appears dry. Fold in eggs before serving.   *Makes 4 servings*

Bean Threads with Minced Pork

Bean Threads with Minced Pork

4 ounces bean threads or Chinese rice vermicelli

3 dried mushrooms

1 small red or green hot chili pepper

3 green onions

2 tablespoons minced fresh ginger

2 tablespoons hot bean sauce

1½ cups chicken broth

1 tablespoon soy sauce

1 tablespoon dry sherry

2 tablespoons vegetable oil

6 ounces lean ground pork

2 cilantro sprigs (Chinese parsley), for garnish

1. Place bean threads and dried mushrooms in separate bowls. Cover each with hot water. Let stand 30 minutes; drain. Cut bean threads into 4-inch pieces. Squeeze out excess water from mushrooms. Cut off and discard stems; cut caps into thin slices.

2. Cut chili pepper in half and scrape out seeds.* Finely mince chili pepper. Thinly slice 2 of the green onions. Cut remaining onion into 1½-inch slivers and reserve for garnish. Combine ginger and hot bean sauce in small bowl. Combine chicken broth, soy sauce and sherry in medium bowl.

*Note: Wear rubber or plastic gloves when cutting chili peppers. Do not touch eyes or lips when handling.

3. Heat oil in wok or large skillet over high heat. Add pork and stir-fry until meat is no longer pink, about 2 minutes. Add chili pepper, sliced onions and ginger-bean sauce mixture. Stir-fry until meat absorbs color from bean sauce, about 1 minute.

4. Add chicken broth mixture, bean threads and mushrooms. Simmer, uncovered, until most of the liquid is absorbed, about 5 minutes. Garnish with onion slivers and cilantro sprigs. *Makes 4 servings*

Fried Rice

3 cups water	2 teaspoons minced fresh ginger
1½ teaspoons salt	8 ounces Barbecued Pork (page 20), cut into thin strips
1½ cups long-grain rice	8 ounces cooked shrimp, shelled, deveined and coarsely chopped
4 slices bacon, chopped	
3 eggs	
⅛ teaspoon pepper	8 green onions, finely chopped
3 tablespoons vegetable oil, divided	1 to 2 tablespoons soy sauce

1. Combine water and salt in 3-quart saucepan. Cover and bring to a boil. Stir in rice; reduce heat, cover and simmer until rice is tender, 15 to 20 minutes; drain.

2. Cook bacon in wok over medium heat, stirring often, until crisp; drain. Remove all but 1 tablespoon bacon drippings from wok.

3. Beat eggs and pepper with fork in small bowl. Pour ⅓ of egg mixture into wok. Tilt wok slightly so egg covers bottom. Cook over medium heat until eggs are set, 1 to 2 minutes. Remove from wok. Roll up omelet and cut into thin strips. Pour ½ tablespoon of the oil into wok. Add ½ of remaining egg mixture; tilt wok and cook until eggs are set. Remove, roll up and cut into thin strips. Repeat with another ½ tablespoon oil and remaining eggs.

4. Heat remaining 2 tablespoons oil in wok over medium-high heat. Add ginger and stir-fry 1 minute. Add rice; cook and stir 5 minutes. Stir in eggs, bacon, pork, shrimp, onions and soy sauce. Cook and stir until heated through. *Makes 6 to 8 servings*

Noodles with Simmered Chicken

4 dried mushrooms
2 teaspoons dry sherry
1 boneless, skinless chicken
    breast half, thinly sliced
1 small bunch watercress or
    ½ bunch fresh spinach leaves
8 ounces Chinese-style thin egg
    noodles

2 cups chicken broth
1 tablespoon soy sauce
¼ cup sliced bamboo shoots
1 teaspoon sesame oil
    Dash ground white pepper
2 green onions, thinly sliced

1. Place mushrooms in bowl and cover with hot water. Let stand 30 minutes. Drain and squeeze out excess water. Cut off and discard stems; cut caps into thin slices.

2. Sprinkle sherry over chicken slices in medium bowl; let stand 15 minutes.

3. Wash watercress and discard thick stems. If using spinach, wash and remove stems; cut into 2-inch wide strips.

4. Cook noodles according to package directions until tender but still firm, 2 to 3 minutes. Drain, rinse under cold running water and drain again.

5. Bring chicken broth and soy sauce to a boil in 3-quart saucepan. Add mushrooms, chicken and bamboo shoots. Reduce heat and simmer, uncovered, about 4 minutes. Add watercress, sesame oil and pepper; simmer 1 minute. Add noodles and cook until heated through.

6. Divide noodles, chicken and vegetables between 2 serving bowls. Ladle broth over noodles. Sprinkle each serving with onions.   *Makes 2 servings*

Note: To store leftover bamboo shoots, place shoots in jar with tight-fitting lid. Add water to cover and seal jar tightly. Bamboo shoots will keep, refrigerated, for up to 10 days, changing water daily.

Steamed Rice

1 cup long-grain rice
2 cups water

1 teaspoon salt
1 tablespoon vegetable oil

1. Place rice in strainer and rinse under cold running water to remove excess starch. Combine rice, water, salt and oil in 3-quart saucepan.

2. Cook over medium-high heat until water boils. Reduce heat to low, cover and simmer until rice is tender, 15 to 20 minutes.

3. Remove from heat; let stand 5 minutes. Uncover and fluff rice lightly with fork.   *Makes 3 cups*

Cold Stirred Noodles

Cold Stirred Noodles

DRESSING
6 tablespoons soy sauce
2 tablespoons sesame oil
¼ cup red wine vinegar

2½ tablespoons sugar
¼ to ½ teaspoon chili oil
(or to taste)

NOODLES
1 pound Chinese-style thin egg
noodles
1 tablespoon sesame oil
2 small carrots, cut into 3-inch
pieces and shredded
3 cups bean sprouts
½ large thin-skinned cucumber,
cut into 3-inch pieces and
shredded

1 bunch radishes, shredded
4 green onions, cut into 2-inch
slivers
1 cup matchstick strips
Barbecued Pork (page 20),
optional

continued page 92

1. Combine all dressing ingredients in small bowl; mix well.

2. Cut noodles into 6-inch pieces. Cook noodles according to package directions until tender but still firm, 2 to 3 minutes. Drain, rinse under cold running water and drain again. Toss noodles with sesame oil until well coated. Refrigerate until ready to serve.

3. Cook carrots in pot of boiling water 30 seconds; drain and rinse under cold running water. Cook bean sprouts in boiling water 30 seconds; drain and rinse under cold running water.

4. To serve, arrange noodles on large platter. Arrange all remaining vegetables and pork on top; sprinkle with onions. Pass dressing separately.

Makes 6 to 8 servings

Vermicelli

8 ounces Chinese rice vermicelli or bean threads **Vegetable oil for frying**

1. Cut bundle of vermicelli in half. Gently pull each half apart into small bunches.

2. Heat oil in wok or large skillet over medium-high heat to 375°F. Using tongs or slotted spoon, lower a small bunch of vermicelli into hot oil. Cook until vermicelli rises to top, 3 to 5 seconds. Immediately remove and drain on paper towels. Repeat with remaining bunches. *Makes about 4 servings*

Fried Noodles

8 ounces Chinese-style thin egg noodles **Salt**
Vegetable oil for frying

1. Cook noodles according to package directions until tender but still firm, 2 to 3 minutes. Drain, rinse under cold running water and drain again.

2. Place several layers of paper towels over cookie sheets or jelly-roll pans. Spread noodles over paper towels and let dry 2 to 3 hours.

3. Heat oil in wok or large skillet over medium-high heat to 375°F. Using tongs or slotted spoon, lower a small portion of noodles into hot oil. Cook until golden, about 30 seconds. Drain on paper towels. Repeat with remaining noodles. *Makes 4 servings*

Index

METRIC CONVERSION CHART

VOLUME MEASUREMENTS (dry)

⅛ teaspoon = 0.5 mL

¼ teaspoon = 1 mL

½ teaspoon = 2 mL

¾ teaspoon = 4 mL

1 teaspoon = 5 mL

1 tablespoon = 15 mL

2 tablespoons = 30 mL

¼ cup = 60 mL

⅓ cup = 75 mL

½ cup = 125 mL

⅔ cup = 150 mL

¼ cup = 175 mL

1 cup = 250 mL

2 cups = 1 pint = 500 mL

3 cups = 750 mL

4 cups = 1 quart = 1 L

VOLUME MEASUREMENTS (fluid)

1 fluid ounce (2 tablespoons) = 30 mL

4 fluid ounces (½ cup) = 125 mL

8 fluid ounces (1 cup) = 250 mL

12 fluid ounces (1½ cups) = 375 mL

16 fluid ounces (2 cups) = 500 mL

WEIGHTS (mass)

½ ounce = 15 g

1 ounce = 30 g

3 ounces = 90 g

4 ounces = 120 g

8 ounces = 225 g

10 ounces = 285 g

12 ounces = 360 g

16 ounces = 1 pound = 450 g

DIMENSIONS

1/16 inch = 2 mm

⅛ inch = 3 mm

¼ inch = 6 mm

½ inch = 1.5 cm

¾ inch = 2 cm

1 inch = 2.5 cm

OVEN TEMPERATURES

250°F = 120°C

275°F = 140°C

300°F = 150°C

325°F = 160°C

350°F = 180°C

375°F = 190°C

400°F = 200°C

425°F = 220°C

450°F = 230°C

BAKING PAN SIZES

Utensil	Size in Inches/ Quarts	Metric Volume	Size in Centimeters
Baking or Cake Pan (square or rectangular)	8 × 8 × 2	2 L	20 × 20 × 5
	9 × 9 × 2	2.5 L	22 × 22 × 5
	12 × 8 × 2	3 L	30 × 20 × 5
	13 × 9 × 2	3.5 L	33 × 23 × 5
Loaf Pan	8 × 4 × 3	1.5 L	20 × 10 × 7
	9 × 5 × 3	2 L	23 × 13 × 7
Round Layer Cake Pan	8 × 1½	1.2 L	20 × 4
	9 × 1½	1.5 L	23 × 4
Pie Plate	8 × 1¼	750 mL	20 × 3
	9 × 1¼	1 L	23 × 3
Baking Dish or Casserole	1 quart	1 L	—
	1½ quart	1.5 L	—
	2 quart	2 L	—